CHOSEN FOR HIS GLORY

A Testimony of Faith and Transformation

Acknowledgements

I would like to express my deepest gratitude to God, whose guidance and blessings have been the foundation of this journey. The Holy Spirit has led me, provided wisdom, and filled my heart with the strength to complete this book. I am eternally grateful for His constant presence and direction throughout my writing process.

I also want to offer my heartfelt thanks to Jesus Christ, whose love and sacrifice have transformed my life. It is in His name that I find true purpose and strength. I am a living testament to His grace and mercy, and I humbly acknowledge that I am His chosen one, created in His image for a divine purpose.

This book is not just a reflection of my personal journey but a testament to the power of faith in Jesus Christ, the Savior. I am thankful for the life and experiences He has given me, and it is my sincere prayer that through these words, others may be inspired to walk in His light and experience the fullness of His love.

To everyone who has supported me, prayed for me, and believed in this vision—thank you from the bottom of my heart. May God continue to bless you all.

In Jesus' name, Amen.

About My Book

This book is not just a collection of words, but a reflection of my own personal journey and experiences. Everything written within these pages comes from my own life, my own practical experiences, and my own faith in Jesus Christ. Each testimony shared is my personal witness, my real-life story of how I have walked in His light, and how He has guided me through every challenge and blessing.

What I have written is a true account of my life—my struggles, my triumphs, and the deep faith that has sustained me. These are not just stories; they are the real-life testimony of how the power of God, through Jesus Christ, has shaped and transformed my existence. My faith has been tested, and through these trials, I have come to understand the true meaning of trust, hope, and love in Him.

This book is not just for the reader to understand my journey, but to inspire others to walk in their own faith, to witness the transformative power of believing in Jesus, and to trust in His plan for each of us. May my story resonate with you and strengthen your own belief, as you too experience the incredible grace of God in your life.

My Desire

My heartfelt desire is that as you read this book, your life will be transformed. Your circumstances will change, and all your dreams and hopes that you have carried in your heart will be fulfilled, in the name of Jesus. I pray that you experience the same strength and blessings that I have received in my life, and that with faith, you too will reach your destined path.

CONTENTS

"He Chose Me"

God chose me. He called me by name, and in His grace, He made me His own. Despite my mistakes, my flaws, and the weight of my sins, He reached out to me. He saved me from the depths of my wrongdoings, forgiving every single error I had made.

With His loving arms, He embraced me, drawing me close to Himself. My Savior, my Messiah, took all my guilt and shame upon Himself, and with His boundless love, He wiped my slate clean.

In that moment, I was no longer the same. He transformed me, healed me, and restored me. He didn't just forgive me—He called me His own, and in doing so, gave me a new life.

"Your Mercy and Grace"
It is by Your mercy, Lord,
By Your kindness that I found life.
You transformed every circumstance,
Turning everything to work in my favor.
There is no enemy, no opposition,
For when You are with me,
Who can stand against me?
What harm can come to me
When You are by my side,
Guiding, protecting, and loving me.

"In the Darkness, You Were With Me"
In the dark, uncertain trials,
You stayed by my side,
Holding my hand through every struggle,
Teaching me the true bond of a Father.
You, O Lord, fulfilled that promise,
Giving me life through Your Son,
And with His precious blood,
You saved me, redeeming my soul.

"From Silence to Hope"
There was a time of silence,
No companion, no friend by my side.
Each moment felt like defeat,
No hope, no destination in sight.
But You chose me,
And gave purpose to my life.
You guided every step I took,
Leading me on the path with Your light,
Walking with me, every step of the way.

"Your Presence in My Darkness"
Whenever I felt all alone,
It was then that I sensed Your presence.
In my moments of sorrow,
Your words gave me strength.
You mended my broken hopes,
And fulfilled every dream within me.
Every moment, my Jehovah,
You were by my side.
There was a time when I felt I had nothing,
But when I found You, I gained everything.
You became the light of my life,
Guiding me through the darkest paths.
You listened to every word I said,
And made them come true.
Like a father fulfilling a child's joy,
You cared for my desires even more.
You, O Lord, surpassed every expectation,
And gave me a life full of grace.

"Surrendering My Burdens to You"
I place all my worries upon You,
All my burdens, I lay at Your feet, my God.
You give me comfort and rest,
You grant me peace,
And You provide me with a life of tranquility.
In You, I find true peace and joy.

"Chosen and Found: My Life with God in Christ"

He chose me. He found me.

I often reflect on this, how, in the midst of my struggles, doubts, and fears, God reached out and found me when I wasn't even looking. I didn't deserve it, yet He chose me. In His grace, He lifted me up from the depths of uncertainty and gave me a new life.

It was as though, one moment, I was lost and drifting, and the next, I was seen, understood, and loved beyond measure. He didn't wait for me to be perfect, or to have all the answers. He found me just as I was, in the midst of my mess, and embraced me with a love that transformed everything.

Through Christ, I became a new creation. The old me, with all my mistakes and brokenness, was replaced with something beautiful, something filled with hope and purpose. It's as if He painted a new world for me, one where I could finally breathe, find peace, and truly live.

He found me when I was lost, and in finding me, He gave me a purpose I never could have imagined. Now, every step I take is guided by His love and grace. I know that I am not alone, that He walks beside me, leading me toward a future filled with promise.

This is the story of how God chose me, how He found me in the deepest parts of my soul, and how He made me new. It's not just a story—it's my life, a life forever changed by His love.

At the time, I didn't know the path of truth or even where it would lead. But God, in His mercy, sent His Son, Jesus Christ, as a sacrifice for us. Through His sacrifice, we were redeemed and our lives saved.

My life took a turn for the better the moment He chose me. When He selected me, everything else became insignificant. The riches, fame, and status of this world—all the things people chase after—are nothing compared to the level of greatness God has given us.

We, His chosen ones, are like royalty. We are kings and queens because our God is greater than anything this world can offer. No amount of money, fame, or high position can compare to the calling we have in Him. The world may value wealth, but God looks at the heart. It is not wealth or status that defines us, but the fact that we are His chosen. The world may see success through money and titles, but the true power lies in the fact that God has chosen us. He sees us for who we truly are, beyond our outer appearances or worldly accomplishments. No one can change a person's heart through money, but only God has the power to transform hearts and lives.

I was chosen by Him, and that choice gave me a new life—one not defined by the world's standards, but by His will. The world looks at outward appearances, but God looks at the heart. And it is through Him that our lives are truly shaped, not by any earthly measure of success.

Prayer

In the beginning, I didn't know how to pray. I didn't understand the process or how it all worked. I was professionally working as an HR Head, and in the eyes of the world, my position, my status, my wealth, and my rank were the measures of success. The world looked at what we had, the titles we carried, and how much wealth we accumulated. But God, He looks at our hearts. He doesn't see the things the world values; He sees deeper.

Initially, I didn't know much about prayer. My brother, though, was the first one in my family to be chosen. He used to go for prayer meetings. When he came home and shared his experiences, our family didn't understand at first. They objected, saying that we belonged to a different faith and that this was something strange for us. But over time, it became more accepted.

At that point, I thought the testimonies people shared were just stories—maybe they were paying people to stand up and share them. That was my initial thought, because I didn't know the truth yet. I hadn't tasted the reality of it for myself. But when God chose me and I tasted His goodness, I understood what the Bible meant when it says, "Taste and see that the Lord is good."

I didn't know how to pray at first, but I understood one thing: I had to thank God for everything. No matter what the situation, I had to be thankful and not worry. That became my focus. I learned not to be anxious about anything. This simple truth—just trusting God and not worrying—became my anchor.

Through my journey, I slowly started to learn that prayer wasn't about fancy words or rituals; it was about gratitude and trust. It was about knowing that no matter what was going on in my life, I could always turn to God and give thanks. As I began to pray, even if I didn't have the perfect words, I knew one thing: in every moment, I had to be thankful and let go of worry. And that's when I started to feel His presence in my life more than ever before

A Simple Prayer

In the beginning, I didn't know how to pray properly. I wasn't familiar with the complex words or the long prayers that people often spoke. I didn't even know how to express my thoughts and desires to God. But all I knew was that I needed guidance. So, my prayers were simple, straight from my heart.

I would say, "God, please show me the right direction. Give me the right path. Help me know what's right and what's wrong for me." It wasn't much, but it was all I could offer at that time. I didn't try to complicate it; I didn't worry about having the right words. I simply asked God to guide me.

Over time, I began to understand that it wasn't about me having control over the situation. I learned to surrender and trust that God would decide what was best for me. I would pray, "God, you decide what is right for me, what is wrong for me. Do what's best for me." This simple, one-line prayer became the foundation of my communication with Him.

It wasn't the length of my prayer that mattered; it was the sincerity and the trust behind it. I had learned that I didn't need to have all the answers or figure it out on my own. All I had to do was ask for His guidance and trust that He would lead me on the right path. And in doing so, I started to feel His presence more clearly, knowing that He was guiding me every step of the way

The Power of The Words

In the beginning, it felt like everything I said came to life instantly. Whatever I spoke, it seemed to happen right away. If I asked for something, it would unfold before me. It was as though my words held immediate power, and I couldn't help but feel amazed. Every time I spoke, I saw results, and that gave me a sense of awe and wonder. It was as though God was listening so closely and responding to every word.

At first, I didn't fully understand why this was happening. I just knew that when I prayed or even simply spoke my desires, things seemed to fall into place. It felt like I had a connection to something bigger than myself, something divine that was making things work in my favor.

But over time, as I spent more time with God, I began to understand the deeper truth behind it. It wasn't that I had some kind of special power. It was God's hand at work, guiding my words and actions. My prayers were being answered, not because of my strength or ability, but because He was listening and answering in His own perfect timing.

I started to understand that the power of my words wasn't just about speaking things into existence—it was about aligning my heart with God's will. As I grew in my faith, I realized that when my heart was in sync with His, my words had more meaning. I wasn't just speaking into the air, but rather, I was speaking in agreement with His plan for me. And that realization filled me with peace. It wasn't about me controlling the outcome, but about trusting that God was in control. Slowly, the more I understood His ways, the more I could see how He was working through my words, guiding me, and shaping my life. It wasn't just a coincidence—it was the power of God at work.

Trusting God in The Workplace

Throughout my professional journey, God always kept me grounded. No matter where I went or what challenges I faced, He was with me every step of the way. In every meeting, every conversation, and in every decision, God's presence was evident. In the world, people often rely on their own understanding or seek the support of others in their social circles, but we, as His chosen ones, are called to rely on God's wisdom, just as King Solomon did. The Bible tells us that Solomon, the wisest man, always sought God's guidance. Even though he was known for his wisdom, he depended on God, and so should we.

I was working in an organization where I faced a significant challenge. The Facility Director had a problematic attitude towards women. His views and actions were not only wrong but also deeply troubling. I had been working there for a long time, but eventually, the situation became unbearable. The mental and emotional toll was immense. There were constant humiliations in meetings, and I felt like I was being tortured for no reason.

I decided to resign and informed the General Manager, CEO, and Medical Director, sending them an email explaining my decision. I explained that the work environment had become toxic and I couldn't continue working under such circumstances. However, despite everything, no action was taken to address the issue. After I left, the Facility Director called me and threatened to file a case against me for causing financial loss to the company. But I knew the truth. In my department, I had no involvement in financial matters. My role was purely administrative—just managing the salaries, which were processed by the corporate office. It wasn't my responsibility, but he threatened me anyway. I was filled with anger and frustration at that moment, and I didn't know how to respond.

That night, I prayed. I prayed to God and said, "If anyone plans to harm me, You will take care of it. You will bring justice." The Bible promises that He will fight for us. I trusted that God would take care of everything, as He had always done in the past.

The next day, I had a vision: I saw the Facility Director being arrested by the police. I didn't know how this would unfold, but I trusted that God was working behind the scenes. I had left the organization, but I still received a call from the MS (Medical Superintendent). They told me I should have never left, that the staff was upset with my decision, and that the Facility Director was bringing in business and revenue. Even though he was wrong, the owners didn't want to lose the business he was bringing.

I said to the MS, "God will bring justice. This man will not stay here much longer. He will be out in two months." Everyone around me was skeptical, saying that wasn't possible. But I had faith that God would make it happen.

A month later, I received a call: the Facility Director was arrested by the police. The justice that I had trusted God for had come to pass. I didn't have to do anything, and I didn't need to pray for revenge. I simply trusted that God would act in His perfect timing. It turned out that this man, whose actions had caused so much harm, had taken his own life due to the pressure of his wrongdoings, and he was taken to jail.

This experience taught me that God is just. We don't have to fight our battles on our own or seek vengeance. We simply need to trust in His timing and His justice. When we rely on God, He takes care of everything, and His justice prevails. I learned that day that God's ways are higher than our ways, and His timing is always perfect.

Trusting God's Justice

There was a time in my life when everything seemed to be going perfectly. On the outside, everything was in place—my career was thriving, I had a good profile in my area, and life was progressing beautifully. But when it came to character, things started to take a turn I wasn't prepared for. I had heard stories that when a woman succeeds and others can't bear to see it, they start to tarnish her reputation.

In our area, if we looked at things from the world's perspective, I was doing well—everything was seemingly perfect. But when it came to my character being questioned, it became incredibly hard to bear. People can endure many things, but being falsely accused and having your name dragged through the mud is something no one can easily tolerate.

But even in those moments, I held onto the truth that God would never allow harm to come my way when I walked with Him. It was at that time that a man, someone I didn't even know, started spreading false rumors about me. He was like the type of person you see on the streets—ignorant, uncouth, and with a reputation for being low-class. He had a horrible appearance and a worse attitude. He began to spread false rumors about my character, which hurt me deeply. I cried a lot, unable to understand why this was happening.

I couldn't bear the false accusations, but I knew I had to surrender everything to God. I left it all in His hands, knowing that He would take care of it in His own way. The man continued to harass me, and even his mother joined in, saying vile things to me. It was like they were a family of low morals, and they just couldn't stop themselves from causing harm.

There were moments when I thought to myself, "Why do people like this exist?" and in my frustration, I even felt like God should take action and make them pay for their wrongdoings. I thought about justice, how it should be swift and sharp, and how they needed to be stopped. But then, I remembered that vengeance belongs to God, not to me.

I began to let go of my anger and frustration. Every time this person's actions made my blood boil, I would remind myself that God would bring justice in His own time. I stopped dwelling on the wrong and started focusing on trusting God. I knew He would handle it. I let go of my desire for revenge, and I chose to trust that God's justice would prevail.

Years passed, and I moved to a different city after getting married. Life went on, and I let go of the painful memories of that time. Then, one day, I received a call from my mother. She told me that the man who had tormented me had met his end. While engaged in his usual unlawful activities, someone had shot him, and he had died from his injuries.

It was God's justice, and I couldn't deny that. I had forgotten about the situation, but God had not. I had let go of my desire for revenge, trusting that He would handle it, and He did. It was like the Bible says: "Whoever draws the sword will die by the sword." Those who live by violence and deceit eventually face the consequences of their actions.

I never wished for anything bad to happen to him. I had forgiven him long ago, but he had chosen a path of destruction. He never stopped with his bad deeds, and in the end, his choices led to his downfall.

Through it all, I learned that we don't need to fight our battles. We don't need to seek revenge or focus on the wrongdoers. Instead, we must trust that God sees everything and will bring about justice in His perfect timing. And in those moments when life feels unfair, we must remember that God is always in control, and He will never leave us to suffer unjustly

We Are His Heroes

We are the sons and daughters of the Most High God, and He has made us heroes in His eyes. In this world, many people take pride in their earnings, their wealth, and their material possessions. They believe that these things define their value and success. But we, as children of God, have something far more valuable than anything this world can offer. We have the Almighty, our Heavenly Father, who owns everything and controls all things. He is our source of strength, provision, and identity.

The Bible teaches us not to worry about anything. It says, "Do not be anxious about anything, but in everything, by prayer and petition, with thanksgiving, present your requests to God." (Philippians 4:6) We are to be thankful in every circumstance, because as we give thanks, God Himself will make us wealthy—not necessarily in material things, but in the blessings of peace, joy, and His presence. He is our Provider, and there is nothing He cannot do. He is the Creator of the universe, and everything is in His hands. There's a beautiful passage in the Bible that reminds us of God's care for us. Jesus said that not even Solomon, in all his splendor, was dressed like the flowers of the field. "Consider the lilies of the field, how they grow: they neither toil nor spin, yet I tell you that not even Solomon in all his glory was dressed like one of these." (Matthew 6:28-29) God takes care of everything He has created, from the flowers to the birds, and He will take care of us, His most precious creation.

Think about the birds for a moment. Every morning, they leave their nests, not storing food for the future, yet they never go hungry. They trust that God will provide for them daily, and He does. They do not worry about tomorrow, but live freely and fully in the present, knowing that their needs will be met. How much more, then, should we, His children, trust in His provision? If God takes care of the birds, how much more will He take care of us, His sons and daughters? We are God's masterpiece, His finest creation. We are His heroes, not because of what we achieve on our own, but because He has chosen us, equipped us, and called us to be His own. Everything we need has already been provided. God has already done it all for us. We don't need to worry or strive in our own strength, because we are living in the fullness of His provision.

Look at King Solomon, one of the wealthiest and wisest men to ever live. In his kingdom, he had everything—gold, riches, splendor beyond imagination. But despite his immense wealth, he made God his priority. Solomon understood that no matter how much wealth he accumulated, it was nothing without God. His relationship with God was more important than his riches.

We, too, should prioritize God in our lives, knowing that everything else will fall into place. Wealth, success, and material possessions are fleeting, but the love and provision of God are eternal. We don't need to chase after things the world offers when we have God, who is greater than everything. As His children, we are already blessed beyond measure.

So, remember: we are heroes not because of what we have, but because of whose we are. We are God's children, and in Him, we lack nothing. We don't need to worry or stress over the things of this world, because God is taking care of us, just as He does for the birds and the flowers. All we need to do is trust, thank Him, and live in the freedom He provides

Miracles in My Life

There are so many miracles in my life that it's impossible to capture all of them in words. The blessings I've received from God are beyond measure, and I can't even begin to explain how many times He has shown up in ways I never expected. His presence in my life has been constant, His love unfailing, and His miracles countless.

One particular incident stands out that I will never forget. It was one of those moments when I realized just how much God cares for us, even in the small details of life.

I had gone shopping at a showroom one day, and after completing my purchase, I left without thinking much about it. When I got home and was unpacking my things, it suddenly hit me—I had forgotten my ATM card at the billing counter. The showroom was quite far from my house, and panic started to set in. I quickly checked my bag, but it wasn't there. I checked again—nothing.

In that moment, I turned to God. I said a simple prayer in my heart, asking for His help. As I prayed, something prompted me to check my bag again. This time, when I checked a third time, I found the card right there in the bag! It was exactly where I had left it, but I hadn't seen it the first two times.

What struck me the most was that I clearly remembered not taking the card from the billing counter, yet there it was, in my bag, as if God Himself had placed it there. It was a small thing, but it showed me that God is always looking out for us, even in the smallest and most seemingly insignificant moments.

I often find that these kinds of little miracles happen when we least expect them. And it's in these moments that I am reminded that God is with us in every detail of our lives. He knows our needs before we even ask, and He is always at work behind the scenes, taking care of us.

God doesn't want us to worry or be anxious. He doesn't want us to fret over the small things in life, because He is already taking care of them. We are His children, and He promises to provide for us in every way. Whether it's a lost ATM card or a much bigger concern, God is always there, ready to step in and show us His love and provision

Divine Intervention and Restoration

After my marriage, God continued to work wonders in my life, and this time, it wasn't just about me—He extended His grace to my family as well. One of the most beautiful miracles I witnessed was in my husband's life. I never had to tell him to seek God or pray—he was drawn to God on his own. Whenever I would pray, he would quietly come and sit beside me, and before I knew it, he was seeking God on his own. It wasn't forced; it wasn't something I had to encourage. He was chosen by God, just like I was. His journey with God was incredible, and his testimony was profound.

But the miracles didn't stop there. It extended to my family, particularly to my sister-in-law. She was facing a difficult time in her marriage, and I didn't know the full extent of the issue. She had been living with us for a while, along with her young son, and there were tensions between her and her husband. I wasn't aware of the details at first, but after our wedding, she still didn't go back to her home. Her husband had come to pick her up, but for some reason, my in-laws didn't allow them to leave. I didn't know why at the time.

But my husband, with his unwavering faith in God, began to speak up. He said that she should go back to her home, that things would get better, and everything would work out. As the weeks passed, the situation worsened. Eventually, the talks led to a divorce. My mother-in-law insisted that divorce was the only option, but my husband, with his firm belief in God, stood strong. He declared that she would go back to her husband's house, and that things would work out. He didn't give up, he kept declaring that everything would be okay.

A year passed, and things took a drastic turn. My sister-in-law's husband had started to fall deeper into addiction—he began drinking heavily and even sold everything, including their gold, car, bike, and phone, just to feed his addiction. My mother-in-law had almost made up her mind that divorce was inevitable. But my husband never lost hope. He continued to believe that God could restore the situation. He declared that her husband would change, and that God would turn everything around.

And that's exactly what happened. Her husband's family intervened—they removed him from the situation, sent him to a rehabilitation center, and slowly but surely, he overcame his addiction. He became sober, and his life was restored. My sister-in-law and her husband reconciled, and there was no divorce. God had worked His miracle.

Even though my sister-in-law didn't reach out to us directly after all this happened, I knew that God's hand was in every step of the process. Her life had been restored because God had intervened. Her husband had been healed, his addiction was broken, and their marriage was saved.

I learned so much from this experience. It wasn't easy to watch from the sidelines, but it taught me to trust in God's timing and His ability to restore even the most broken situations. My husband's unwavering belief in God's power to heal and restore was a testimony of God's faithfulness.

It reminded me that no matter how impossible a situation may seem, when we place our trust in God, He will bring healing, peace, and restoration.

This was a reminder to me of the power of prayer, faith, and divine intervention. It showed me that with God, nothing is too difficult to overcome. We must trust Him, even when the circumstances seem hopeless, because He is the one who brings life and hope where there seems to be none.

Life in Christ- True Shepherd

In Christ, we find our true Shepherd. He is the source of everything we need, and through Him, we lack nothing. I remember a time when I wasn't in close contact with anyone, but God was always with me. I had a thirst for His Word, a desire to learn more, but there was no one to guide me or teach me at that time. It was a period of spiritual hunger, and both my husband and I were being taught directly by God.

Many people I knew were used to learning from leaders and teachers, thinking that only through them could one grow spiritually. But my husband and I were in a situation where we weren't in close fellowship with anyone, not attending prayer meetings or any gatherings. However, God Himself started teaching us. I realized that God had spoken directly to Abraham, and David didn't have any spiritual leader guiding him either. It's important to understand that God, in His infinite power, can teach anyone—whether through a child or any means He desires. We should never doubt His ability.

God is the ultimate teacher. Yes, it's good to attend prayer meetings and worship, but when there is no one else to guide you, God Himself is the source. As the Bible says, "The Lord is our Shepherd, and He leads us beside still waters." It's through Him that we are taught and guided.

Think about how plants grow. A plant in the wild doesn't receive any direct care, yet it grows and thrives because God sustains it. However, the plants we have in our homes require us to water them regularly. If we neglect them for a few days, they begin to wither and die. In the same way, we cannot depend on others for our spiritual growth all the time. While pastors and leaders can help, we should not rely solely on them. God has created us in His image, and Jesus Himself said, "You will do even greater works than I did." Nowhere does the Bible say that prayer from a pastor is the only way to see change. The Bible teaches that through Christ, we are empowered to do all things. He is our source, and we should depend solely on Him.

When we continuously depend on others for spiritual nourishment, it's like watering a plant that doesn't have strong roots. A plant that grows by itself, with deep roots, is resilient and can withstand any storm. It's the same with our faith. If we keep depending on others, we never develop the strength and maturity we need to stand firm on our own. It's like learning to ride a bicycle. If someone holds the bike while you learn, you will always be dependent on them. But once you let go and gain confidence, you will be able to ride freely, at your own pace, without fear.

The same principle applies to our walk with God. How long will we depend on others to teach us? Instead, we should tell God, "Lord, teach me Yourself." As my hunger for God grew, He began teaching me directly through His Spirit. It was a personal experience, and as my desire for His Word increased, I learned more and more directly from Him. This is the life in Christ—a life of direct, personal relationship with the Creator. When we depend on Him, He leads us, teaches us, and empowers us to live the life He has planned for us.

In Him, we lack nothing. He is our Shepherd, and He will lead us through every situation, teaching us all the way. Let us not depend on others but on Him alone, for He is the source of our strength, our wisdom, and our purpose

God, Our Protector and Caregiver

God holds us as the apple of His eye. He watches over us with the utmost care, like a parent cherishing their most precious child. In the same way that the eye is protected by the eyelid, God protects us. His love and care for us are so deep that He has written our names on the palms of His hands, and He calls us His masterpiece.

Have you ever experienced something in your eye, and instinctively, your eyelid blinks, swiftly removing it? That is the level of care God has for us. Just as the eyelid protects the eye, God steps in quickly to protect us whenever there is danger or trouble. He ensures that we are safe and that nothing harms us. Even when we are unaware, He is watching over us, ensuring that we are saved from every danger.

The Bible says, "I will never leave you nor forsake you" (Hebrews 13:5). God's presence with us is constant. He is always with us, watching over us, guiding us, and protecting us. His love is unwavering, and His commitment to our well-being is eternal.

I recall an experience my husband and I had once while we were on our way to fellowship. We were riding on a bike together, and on one side of the road, there was a tractor trolley, and on the other side, a drainage ditch. Out of nowhere, a cyclist came from the opposite side, and in an attempt to avoid him, we lost control and crashed. The bike, a sports bike, was quite heavy, and it fell on my left leg with tremendous force. I remember the impact was so strong that all I could say was, "Thank God for saving us." When we fell, we landed on the dirt side of the road. As I got up, I felt intense pain in my leg, but my first thought was to thank God. The weight of the bike had fallen directly on my leg, and I could feel the strain. But I immediately prayed and said, "Lord, You care for my bones and my body. Please don't let anything happen to me." Miraculously, when I checked my leg, there was no serious injury. The pain gradually faded, and my leg was completely fine.

This experience was a powerful reminder of how God truly takes care of us. We might not always see it, but God is always at work, even in moments of distress. He cares for us more deeply than we can understand. Just like how our eyelid protects our eye in an instant, God is always there, stepping in to safeguard us from harm.

God's care for us goes beyond anything we can comprehend. He is always watching, always protecting, and always making sure that we are safe in His arms. Even in the most difficult situations, when things seem uncertain or dangerous, we can trust that God is with us, guiding us, and protecting us. Just as He promises in His Word, He will never leave us or forsake us.

His protection is not limited to physical safety. He watches over our emotional well-being, our thoughts, our hearts, and our every need. Like a parent who knows when their child needs help before they ask, God is aware of everything happening in our lives, and He acts to protect us, even when we don't realize it.

Let this truth comfort you today: God is the One who keeps you safe, who watches over you with the most tender love, and who will never leave you. You are His precious child, and He cares for you deeply, more than you can ever imagine

Asking in Faith

One day, my husband and I were praying and sharing our thoughts with each other. He had a question that was on his heart: "Is it really necessary to ask God for what we need? The Bible says, 'Ask and it will be given to you,' but what does that mean? Why do we need to ask? God is our Father, and He already knows our needs. He can give us everything we need, so why do we have to ask?"

At that moment, my husband was feeling a little bit discouraged, unsure about why asking was so important. But God, in His wisdom, began to teach him the answer. I explained to him, using an analogy that helped clarify the situation.

I told him, "Imagine a small child who is hungry. Even though the mother knows the child is hungry, she doesn't just place food in front of the child without the child asking. The child needs to express their need and ask for food. The mother, of course, knows the child is hungry, but the act of asking is part of the relationship. The child asks, and the mother gives. This is how it works with God. He knows our needs, but He wants us to ask, because asking is part of our relationship with Him."

I went on to share a personal story. I remember a time when I had admired a beautiful gold ring. My father was traveling to Dubai, and before he left, I told him, "I would like a gold ring, one from Dubai, because the gold there is really good." When my father returned, he didn't waste any time. The moment he arrived, before even having a drink of water or resting, he took the ring out of his bag and gave it to me. This act of love and care showed me how much my father loved me. He didn't hesitate to fulfill my request because he loved me and wanted to make me happy.

This is how God, our Father, is with us. He loves us deeply, and just as my father gave me the ring I asked for, God is ready and willing to provide for all our needs—whether physical, material, or spiritual. He wants us to ask, not because He doesn't know what we need, but because asking strengthens our relationship with Him.

I also explained, "Just as a child has no doubt that their parents will provide, we should also have that same childlike faith when we ask God for something. A child, when they need something, doesn't worry about how it will come or who will provide it. They just tell their parents, and then they rest in the assurance that their needs will be met. They don't need to know how it will happen or when; they simply trust that their parents will take care of it."

In the same way, we should approach God with that kind of trust and faith. We should bring our needs and desires to Him, and then leave them in His hands. It is not about begging or pleading; it is about knowing our rights as His children and trusting that He will provide for us. God has already promised that He will take care of us. Our responsibility is to ask with faith, trusting that He will respond in His perfect timing and way.

When we ask God, it's not about worrying or doubting how it will happen. We don't need to stress about the "how" or the "when." Just as a child tells their parents what they need and trusts that their parents will take care of it, we should do the same with God. We tell Him our needs, and then we rest in His faithfulness.

God also wants us to approach Him not just for material things, but for spiritual needs as well. Just as a child grows in their learning and understanding, God is ready to give us wisdom, guidance, and spiritual growth. He wants to equip us with everything we need to live a godly life. When we ask for spiritual gifts or for help in our walk with Him, He will provide.

God's responsibility is to provide for us. Our responsibility is to ask and trust. When we ask, we are acknowledging that He is our source, that we are dependent on Him, and that we trust His provision. God's love for us is so great that He will not withhold anything good from us. Whether it's something material, emotional, or spiritual, He is faithful to provide when we ask with a sincere heart.

So, when you find yourself in need, don't hesitate to ask God. Ask with faith, with the confidence that He is your loving Father, and that He is more than able to meet all your needs. And when you ask, rest in His peace, knowing that He will take care of everything

God's Plans Are Greater

The thoughts we carry in our minds, the desires we have in our hearts, sometimes seem so important to us. But little do we know that God's plans for us are far beyond what we could ever imagine. As it is written in His Word, "For I know the plans I have for you, declares the Lord, plans to prosper you and not to harm you, plans to give you a hope and a future" (Jeremiah 29:11). Our own understanding is limited, but God's vision for us is limitless, and His plans for our lives are filled with beauty and purpose.

There are times when we may feel uncertain or frustrated because the things we desire don't seem to be falling into place. It might feel like we've made certain plans in our minds, but they haven't materialized the way we expected. But take heart, because God's plans for you are much greater than your own. His plans are perfect, and they are designed with your ultimate good in mind.

You are chosen. You are part of a royal lineage. As believers, we are heirs to the Kingdom of God. We are His children, and He has made us royalty in His sight. He has chosen us to be part of His glorious family. You might not always see it, but God has set aside a unique, beautiful destiny for each of us, a plan that is far greater than anything we could ever imagine.

Think about it. We serve an all-powerful, almighty God— the Creator of the universe, the One who spoke everything into existence. The same God who holds the world in His hands, who created the stars and the oceans, has a plan specifically for you. This God, the sovereign Lord, is the one who has already prepared amazing things for you. His plans for you are not just good, but magnificent, filled with grace, favor, and blessings beyond your comprehension.

Imagine what beautiful things God has set aside for you. His love for you is so deep that He has prepared a life for you that is full of hope, purpose, and fulfillment. The desires of your heart, the dreams you've been carrying, are not far from His plans. He is working all things together for your good. Even when it feels like things aren't going the way you want, trust that God's plan is unfolding in ways that you may not yet understand.

We might be limited by our understanding of time and circumstances, but God is not bound by those limitations. He sees the bigger picture, and He is working behind the scenes, orchestrating everything for our benefit. He is the sovereign God, the One who can turn any situation around and bring about His perfect will.

So, when you face challenges or disappointments, remember that God's plans for you are far greater than anything you could have imagined. He is working things out in your favor, even when you can't see it. Trust that His timing is perfect and that He is leading you toward something beautiful and fulfilling.

As His children, we are not destined for ordinary lives. We are part of His royal family. We are heirs to His Kingdom, and He has prepared a magnificent future for us. Think about the beauty and the greatness of what God has in store for you. His plans for your life are far beyond your own thoughts and dreams. Keep your trust in Him, knowing

that He is the one guiding you toward the most wonderful future, filled with blessings, love, and hope.
God's plans are greater than our own, and He has something so beautiful and perfect prepared for each of us. So, hold on to hope, trust in His perfect plan, and know that His thoughts toward you are good. You are chosen, and you are loved, and He has incredible things waiting for you

Doing Everything for God's Glory

In every task we do, big or small, we should approach it with gratitude and a heart of worship. Whether we are working at home, in the office, or serving in any capacity, it is important to remember that we are doing it not just for ourselves but for God. As the Bible teaches, "Whatever you do, work at it with all your heart, as working for the Lord, not for human masters" (Colossians 3:23).

There may be moments when the work seems tiring, overwhelming, or even frustrating. We might feel like complaining, or perhaps we struggle to see the value in what we're doing. But in those moments, we must remind ourselves that God sees everything we do. When we work, we do it as a service to Him, not for the praise of others or the recognition of the world.

Complaining or grumbling while working not only drains our energy but also takes away from the purpose behind the work. It shifts our focus from gratitude to frustration. Instead, if we do our work with a thankful heart, acknowledging that God has placed us in that position and trusting that He will use it for His glory, we will find that our work becomes more fulfilling and meaningful.

When we do something, no matter how small or routine, and we do it with the intention of honoring God, we invite His blessing into that task. There is a special kind of blessing that comes when we approach our work with a heart of thanksgiving. As we give thanks to God for the opportunity to work, we open the door for His favor to flow into everything we do.

This doesn't mean that every task will be easy or without challenges, but when we choose to do everything in God's name and with gratitude, we invite His presence into that task. He gives us strength, joy, and peace, even in difficult situations, and He promises to bless the work of our hands when we do it for His glory.

Think about the work of a gardener who tends to the plants and flowers. When the gardener cares for each plant with love and patience, that care is reflected in the beauty of the garden. Similarly, when we approach our work with love and dedication, knowing that we are working for God, it will bear fruit—whether it's the fruit of skill, fulfillment, or even the blessing of others who are touched by our efforts.

When we begin each task with the intention to honor God and give thanks for the ability to do it, we open ourselves up to experiencing God's presence in every part of our lives. It's not just about completing the task—it's about the attitude we bring to it. Work done with gratitude becomes an act of worship.

So, let's remember that in everything we do, we are serving the Lord. Whether it's a mundane task or a challenging project, let's do it with a heart full of thanksgiving. By honoring God in all our work, we allow His blessing to flow, and our work becomes more than just an obligation—it becomes a meaningful expression of worship.

As the Bible reminds us, "In everything, give thanks" (1 Thessalonians 5:18). This is how we invite God's presence into our daily lives and make every task, no matter how simple, a reflection of His glory

The Power of Our Words

As I reflect on the words I've often heard, especially from older generations, I am struck by how powerful our words can be—both for good and for bad. One of the most concerning things I've witnessed is how many parents, particularly mothers, speak negatively to and about their own children. I've often heard mothers telling their daughters, "You never know what kind of people you will meet after marriage," or, "Live your life now because who knows what will happen tomorrow? You never know what kind of troubles you might face." These words may seem harmless at first, but they carry so much weight.

By saying these things, these parents are unintentionally declaring curses over their children's future. They are reinforcing fear and negativity instead of speaking hope and life. It's as if they are preparing their children for failure, saying, "You may face difficulties, and things might not go well for you." When these things eventually happen—when the daughter doesn't find a good family after marriage or faces challenges in her relationships— parents wonder, "Why did this happen to my child? What wrong did we do?" The truth is, by speaking such negative things into existence, they have, in a sense, invited those very struggles into their lives.

We must realize that words carry tremendous power. In Christ, our words are not just mere expressions; they hold authority. The Bible teaches us that the tongue has the power of life and death (Proverbs 18:21). We can either speak life and blessings over our children and others, or we can speak destruction and curses without even realizing it. We are responsible for the words we speak because they shape not only our lives but also the lives of those around us.

When we speak negativity, we are sowing seeds of doubt, fear, and curses. But when we speak faith, encouragement, and hope, we are sowing seeds of blessings and victory. In Christ, we are called to bless and not to curse. Our words should reflect the goodness of God, not the fear and doubt of the world.

For example, instead of telling our children, "Live it up now, because you never know what tomorrow holds," we can tell them, "You are blessed, and God has great plans for your life. He will lead you through every challenge, and He will bring you into a future full of peace and joy. Trust in His guidance." Instead of saying, "Who knows what will happen after marriage?" we can say, "God has a good plan for your future, and He will bring people into your life who will bless and support you."

We need to encourage our children to trust God, to believe in His goodness, and to have faith that He will provide for them. We should remind them that they are not alone, and that their heavenly Father will take them to places beyond their imagination. It's so important to empower them with words that uplift and inspire.

As parents, we must be careful with the messages we send. We should speak life and blessings over our children, reminding them that they are loved by God and that He is their ultimate guide. We should never instill fear or doubt in their hearts by telling them that their future is uncertain or that they might face hardship. Instead, we should assure them that God is with them, and that He will make a way where there seems to be no way.

In the same way, we must speak blessings over others. Let's choose to speak words that build others up, that give them hope, and that point them to the truth of God's love and provision. Instead of cursing or condemning, we are called to bless, to encourage, and to inspire.

Remember, the words we speak have the power to shape our futures and the futures of those around us. So, let's choose to speak words of life, to declare blessings over our children, our families, and ourselves. Let's be mindful of the power of our words and use them to build a future that reflects the goodness of God. Speak blessings, not curses. Speak life, not death. And watch how God will use your words to create a beautiful and victorious future.

Living in God's Command

Many times, I found myself pondering the meaning of walking in God's Word. What does it truly mean to follow His commandments? Does it simply mean to adhere to the words and teachings, or does it go deeper, transforming who I am? I often asked myself: how does one live in complete obedience to His will?

In search of answers, I turned to God, the ultimate source of life. I asked Him, "Father, teach me how to live in Your commandments. How can I follow You fully?" It was then that He spoke into my heart, revealing a profound truth: to walk in His commandments, I first needed to empty myself, much like an empty vessel. Only when I am empty can He fill me.

God instructed me to approach Him with a heart free of preconceived notions, like an empty cup ready to be filled. If I walked with my own thoughts, beliefs, and biases, I would not be able to receive the fullness of His teachings. Instead, I needed to come to Him with a clean and open heart. When I approached God in this way, He could pour His wisdom and guidance into my life.

This revelation reminded me of the image of a goat, which is active while alive, but when it dies, its skin can be used to make a drum (Tabla,dholak), which produces sound when struck. Similarly, when we live with our own will and ego, we are constantly active in our own ways. But when we surrender to God, we are transformed, and His voice becomes the one that guides us.

God also showed me the importance of not relying on societal norms or expectations. It's not about following what the world says but trusting in God's guidance. I learned that God wants us to cleanse our hearts and minds from all negativity. He taught me to let go of any conflicts or resistance in my heart. By maintaining a pure heart, free from bitterness or pride, we can walk in harmony with God. There was a time when I struggled with feelings of male dominance and oppression in my surroundings. This caused me distress, and I turned to my husband to discuss these feelings. After that, I brought the matter before God. He taught me that to live in peace, I must focus solely on Him. My heart needed to be entirely dedicated to Him and not to the distractions of the world.

God revealed that living a life of complete devotion means keeping your mind and heart focused on Him, free from any distractions or emotional baggage. When we walk in this way, with pure hearts and minds, God's presence and guidance are always with us.

Ultimately, I realized that living according to God's commandments isn't about following rules or doing things for the sake of tradition; it is about surrendering ourselves to Him, cleansing our hearts, and allowing Him to guide our lives. When we walk in His ways with pure intent, He walks with us

Perception is Reality - Our Response to Life's Challenges

In life, circumstances are nothing but a reflection of our thoughts. It's not the situation itself that defines us but how we perceive it. "Perception is reality" – what you perceive to be true is what will manifest in your life. This principle has shaped my understanding and approach to life. The key to navigating through challenges lies in maintaining a positive perception.

Our thoughts shape our reality. The way we perceive a situation dictates how we experience it. When we shift our mindset, we shift our reality. Conditions themselves are not the problem; it is our perception of those conditions that determine the outcome. If we think negatively, the situation will seem negative. But if we choose to look at things with optimism, the outcome will also shift accordingly.

I have personally experienced the power of perception and response in a real-life situation. There was once an incident when my company outsourced some work to another party. We were the first party, and they were the second. Due to the poor quality of their services, we decided to discontinue the partnership after several reminders. But to my surprise, they sent a legal notice in my name, demanding some reimbursement. I was told they would take action against us.

Now, most people would panic or stress over such a situation, but I was unfazed. I wasn't bothered by it at all.

In fact, I didn't even react. Why? Because I knew that I didn't need to worry. I knew that God was on my side, and He would fight my battles for me. I didn't need to get involved in the stress.

When I received the notice, I simply looked at it and said, "This is just a waste of paper." I didn't let it bother me. I then consulted with my lawyer, and in the end, the matter was resolved. Nothing came out of it. Why? Because my perception was different from others'. While others may have seen it as a problem, I saw it as nothing more than a minor bump in the road.

This experience taught me a valuable lesson: How we react to situations determines their outcome. If I had panicked or reacted negatively, I would have made the situation more stressful than it needed to be. But by remaining calm and choosing not to react, I allowed the situation to resolve itself.

This is exactly what God teaches us in our walk with Him. We are followers of Christ, and our identity is in Him. Christ never feared any situation, so why should we? The power lies in how we respond. It's not the circumstances themselves that matter, but how we react to them.

Most people panic because they attribute the fear to the situation itself. They say, "The situation is difficult; I'm scared." But in reality, it is our own perception that creates fear. We make situations bigger in our minds than they actually are. If we choose to take a step back and see the situation as nothing more than a temporary challenge, we will not let it overwhelm us.

Just as Christ did not fear, we must also learn not to fear. He is with us, and He will guide us through any challenge. Life will throw curveballs, but how we perceive and react to them is what defines us. So, remember: **circumstances are nothing; it's our perception that matters.**

Take every challenge lightly, knowing that God is on your side. When we choose to trust in Him and view situations with His perspective, we will always come out victorious

Everything Works Together for Your Good

In life, everything that happens, no matter how it seems in the moment, is ultimately working for your good. Even the challenges, the delays, the setbacks—all of them are part of a greater plan that is leading you to a better place. There is a profound truth that we need to embrace: **everything, when seen through the lens of faith, is shaping and refining you for your highest good.**

Sometimes, we find ourselves experiencing delays in life— whether it's a project, a goal, or something we've been working toward. But we must understand one thing clearly: **any delay is never from God.** God is never the source of delay in our lives. His timing is always perfect, and He works on our behalf swiftly and precisely. When we experience delays, it's not because God is withholding something from us—it's because we may not be stable in our thoughts, beliefs, or actions.

You see, delays happen when we are not consistent in our mindset, when we are not confident in our beliefs, or when we are not aligned with our vision. **When we are unstable in our thoughts, when we are uncertain about our goals,**

or when our faith wavers, we create the conditions for delay. This is not God's doing, but a reflection of our own inner state.

For instance, if we lack confidence in what we are doing or if we doubt the outcome, it creates an internal resistance. We may not be fully aligned with our purpose, and in those moments of uncertainty, it feels like nothing is moving forward. But the truth is, **we have the power to overcome delays simply by being stable and confident in our actions and beliefs**.

It's essential to stay grounded in your faith and in the belief that everything is working out for your good. When you are sure of your goal, sure of your purpose, and confident in your abilities, nothing can hold you back. If you remain stable in your belief, your thoughts, and your actions, the so-called delays will disappear, and everything will come together in God's perfect timing.

Think about it—how often have you experienced a delay, only to realize later that it was a blessing in disguise? Perhaps the delay gave you time to refine your plan, to strengthen your skills, or to clarify your vision. Maybe what you thought was a delay was actually God preparing you for something greater. God is always working behind the scenes, moving with such speed and precision that, in the blink of an eye, He can turn things around.

When we stay confident in God's plan and remain stable in our beliefs, we allow Him to work in us and through us. **God works at the speed of thought.** His ability to bring things into reality is faster than we can imagine. The key is to trust Him and to be steady in our own actions and beliefs.

If you are not confident in what you are doing, if you are unsure about your goals, how can anyone else be certain for you? It is not the fault of others when things don't move forward—it's about our own confidence, focus, and stability. **When you trust God's timing and remain anchored in faith, no delay will keep you from your destiny.**

So, remember this: **all things are working together for your good**, even when it doesn't seem like it. Delays are not a punishment, and they are not from God. They are simply opportunities for us to strengthen our resolve, build our faith, and trust that God is moving faster than we can perceive. **Stay stable, stay confident, and trust in God's perfect plan**

A Transformed Life in Christ

When I gave my life to Christ, everything changed. My lifestyle, my mindset, and the way I responded to life's challenges were completely transformed. One of the most significant changes was that I stopped reacting negatively to situations. Before, I would quickly get angry, frustrated, or upset by the smallest things. But now, my approach to life is different. Now, when something happens, I pause and ask myself, **"What would Jesus do in this situation?"** This question has become a guide for me. I remember that **my identity is in Christ**. He lives in me, and I walk with His presence in my life every single day. I carry His spirit with me, and I strive to reflect His love, grace, and patience in every situation. **Christ is in me, and I walk in His footsteps.** Before I gave my life to Christ, if someone said something hurtful, I would instantly feel anger rise up within me. I would respond harshly, maybe even lash out. But now, I know better. Instead of reacting with anger, I choose to bless those who hurt me. I speak blessings instead of curses. I no longer let negativity control me.

I used to get angry when stuck in traffic. If someone cut me off or did something that irritated me, I would shout, curse, or complain. But now, I understand that my words have power. **I have the power to choose how I respond, and I choose peace and patience.** I speak life, not death. I speak blessings, not curses.

Today, I walk in the strength and authority that comes from Christ. My words are no longer just words—they carry weight. They carry His power. **In His strength, I am able to stay calm, even in situations that once would have triggered anger or frustration.** This power is not from me; it is His power in me. And I am learning to use that power for good.

When I think about the way I used to react, I realize how far I have come. **In Christ, I am a new creation, and my old ways of reacting have been replaced by His love and wisdom.** Now, I ask myself, "How would Jesus respond?" and I seek to live out His example in my everyday actions.

It's amazing to see how Christ's presence changes everything. I no longer feel controlled by my emotions or circumstances. I am learning to walk in His peace, His patience, and His love. And the most beautiful part is that **His power is in me, and it allows me to live differently— more peacefully, more lovingly, and with greater purpose.**

Life in Christ: The Power of Our Words
In our journey with Christ, we must be mindful of the words we speak. Every word we utter is like a seed, and what we speak will grow into reality. The power of speech is not to be taken lightly. God has given us authority in this vast universe, and what is greater than that which He has granted us? We are empowered by the Spirit of victory; we are called to live as conquerors.

Our words carry authority, and whatever we declare will come to pass. That is why we must never speak negatively. We should not speak harmful words about our health, our work, or even our children. Every morning when we wake up, let us thank God for the blessing of life. Speak words of faith and gratitude. Remember, the authority that God has given us can create life or bring destruction. So, let us choose to speak words that bring life, health, and blessings.

The Power of Words: Transforming Lives
Words have power—power that can transform lives. The words we speak are not just sounds; they carry immense potential to shape our reality. With each word, we create something. Words can heal, uplift, and build, or they can harm, destroy, and tear down.

This power comes from God, who has granted us the ability to speak life into our situations. Through our words, we can declare victory, success, and peace, or we can invite negativity, fear, and defeat. It is important to realize that what we speak has the ability to change our lives.

When we speak with faith and wisdom, we align ourselves with God's purpose for our lives. Let us be careful with the words we choose, for in them lies the power to change our world and our destiny. Speak life, speak hope, and speak faith. Through the power of your words, you have the ability to transform not just your own life, but also the lives of those around you.

Speaking Life over Every Situation

The things that are unseen, the promises of God, He calls them as though they already are. Just as God speaks life into the invisible, we too should speak faith into our lives. Whatever you desire to see, speak it into existence. If you want a good life, declare it. Speak words that align with the future you want, not the circumstances that may be in front of you today.

If you're facing a challenge or negative situations, don't speak what you see; speak what you believe. Speak positivity over your life, over your health, and your future. If things aren't going the way you want, declare, *"All is well, and good things are coming."* If you face rejection, say, *"This rejection is a redirection to something better!"* If things feel like they're falling apart, speak faith, *"This is leading to my success and breakthrough."*

When you speak words of faith and confidence, every situation will begin to work in your favor. You have the power to declare that every setback is a setup for your comeback. Speak life, speak hope, and speak victory, for as you speak, so shall it be. Your words are the building blocks of your future. Choose them wisely, and speak with authority.

Practical Steps for Speaking Life and Living with Purpose

Start speaking the things you desire, even when you don't yet see them in your life. If you want a good career, declare that you already have it. Speak with faith, and begin living practically in alignment with your words. If you're a young person aiming for success, start believing that your future is already secure, that you are capable of achieving everything you desire.

Too often, people speak negatively about themselves, their country, or their situation. They don't realize how powerful their words are. Instead of speaking negativity, speak positivity. Declare over your life: *"I am doing well. My career is thriving. My business is flourishing. My city is the best. My country is the best. My life is blessed, and my children are great."*

Declare these things every day, especially in your prayers. Speak life over your relationships, your career, and your circumstances. Too many people focus on negative news and speak out of fear or frustration. Don't let that be you. Speak what you want to see, not what you don't want to see.

In practical life, discipline is key. Without discipline, you won't see results. The Bible tells us that when Moses and the Israelites were stuck at the Red Sea with the Egyptian army behind them, the people started complaining. God told Moses to command them to be quiet. Why? Because in times of trouble, when we stay quiet and control our words, we allow God to move and our situations to change. Controlling your words is a powerful practice. Just as David prayed, *"Lord, set a guard over my mouth; keep watch over the door of my lips."* The tongue is like a fire, and it can either build up or destroy. Be intentional about your words and guard them carefully. When you speak with faith and discipline, even the most difficult situations will change for the better.

Practical steps for you:

- Speak life every day. Declare positive things over your life and your future.
- Focus on what you want to see and speak those things into existence.
- Be disciplined with your words—don't speak in frustration or negativity.
- Quiet your mind in tough situations and trust that your words of faith will bring change.
- Apply consistency and action in your life to back up your words with practical steps.

Testimony of God's Presence in Our Professional Lives

There are times in life when we encounter people who make it difficult to deal with, especially in our professional journeys. But in my experience, I've always made it a point to put God first in my work, and through His grace, I have seen my work flourish. I have a personal testimony to share from 15-16 July 2022. It was a time of inspection in my organization, and I had only been appointed as the unit head a few months before. I have 11 years of experience in this particular field, but at that moment, I was made to feel inferior. The group head made a sarcastic comment, questioning my abilities and saying I didn't know much about the work.

Many professionals try to project themselves as superior, boasting about their knowledge or connections, while trying to belittle others. They fail to realize that our true identity comes not from what we know or who we know, but from the Creator of the universe, who is in control of everything. I just prayed, "Lord, I trust that You will lift me up. I know You won't let me be shamed in front of others."

The inspection began with a team from Delhi's board, and there was an assessor there with whom I had worked on previous assessments at another organization. I mentioned that I knew her, but the group head mocked me, saying that's not how it works. The inspection continued for two full days, and during the final review and presentation, I sat in the second row, trusting in God's plan for me. I prayed again, "Lord, you promised that You would honor me today, in front of everyone."

And then, to my surprise, the assessor pointed at me and said, *"This girl, the head of HR, she is very good at what she does. I have met with her 2-3 times, and her department is doing very well."* She praised me in front of the entire room. That moment was a powerful reminder of how God honors His children.

The assessor then told the group head, *"Your department is weak."* After the meeting, the group head approached me and said, *"That was a big deal. She appreciated you in front of everyone."* This was nothing short of God's favor. He never lets us be ashamed, and He always lifts us up when we place our trust in Him.

There was another time, about 5-6 years ago, when a similar situation occurred in another organization. The CEO had commented that my department was "zero." In that moment, I boldly responded, *"If my department is zero, then take the Z off and make it H!"* The reality was that the performance of my department turned out to be so excellent that people were saying, *"She is the pillar. She is the hero."* This was only by God's grace and favor.

In your professional life, if anyone tries to make you feel inferior, don't accept it. We are not inferior; we are superior, because God, our Father, is with us. Never let anyone make you feel less than what you are in Christ. With God, we are always victorious, always able to rise above challenges, and always positioned for success.

Let these experiences remind you that when you place your trust in God and take Him with you into every meeting, every task, He will honor you and show you favor. You are His child, and He will never let you be ashamed.

Testimony of Healing: Trusting God in Moments of Health Crisis

I want to share a personal testimony about God's healing power in my life. One early morning, around 3 AM, I woke up to go to the washroom. Suddenly, I began feeling dizzy, and my health rapidly deteriorated. The heat from the summer was intense, and as I stood there, I began to lose my balance. I started to feel weak, and soon, I could barely walk back to my room.

I felt a wave of fear, but I immediately began to pray. I said, "Lord, You are my Savior, my Healer. You are the One who holds me in Your hands. I trust You, and I know nothing will happen to me." As I struggled to make it back to my room, I called out to my mother for help and collapsed onto the bed. My body started shivering, and I felt numbness in my hands and feet. My breathing became difficult, and my heart rate skyrocketed.

My parents, brother, and husband began to pray for me. They called a doctor, who came and checked me. I had a fever of 104°F, which was incredibly dangerous, especially in the hot weather. I started to lose consciousness, and my blood started to clot in my palms. My family continued to pray, and my brother spoke to me, trying to remind me to stay strong. He said, "Listen to me, you are okay. You are fine."

Even though I could barely speak or move, I felt a still small voice in my spirit telling me, *"You are fine. You will get through this."* Even though my body felt numb and I could hardly move, my focus was on God and His power. Slowly, after some time, I regained consciousness, but I couldn't get up. I commanded myself in Jesus' name, *"I am healed, I am fine!"* and slowly began to move. With determination, I walked to the sofa and sat down.

My father suggested I rest on the bed, but my spirit knew I had to keep moving. I stood firm in my authority and commanded my body to obey. Within moments, my health began to stabilize. The dizziness, numbness, and discomfort began to fade.

This experience taught me an important lesson: When we speak with authority and believe that we are healed, our bodies respond. We cannot let sickness or negative circumstances dictate how we feel. By commanding our bodies in faith, we align ourselves with God's healing power. No sickness or disease has the power to overcome us because we have the spirit of victory living inside us.

Always speak life over your health. Even in the toughest moments, remember that you have the authority to command your body, your health, and your life. Trust in God's promises and know that He is your Healer. When you speak with faith and authority, nothing can hold you back from the healing and health that God has already provided for you.

Testimony of Strength through God's Presence

I was never in fear, but the moment God chose me, He made me even stronger. My strength didn't come from myself, but from Him. I placed all my circumstances before Him, and He empowered me to face everything with confidence and resilience. God gave me the strength to rise above every challenge and helped me to stand firm in the face of adversity.

It's His presence that has made me unshakable. I remember a powerful verse: *"Do not fear, for I am with you; do not be dismayed, for I am your God. I will strengthen you and help you; I will uphold you with my righteous right hand."* This verse reminded me that no matter what happens, I am never alone.

Though I never felt afraid, He made me even stronger. His power and guidance kept me steady, and I found that with each challenge, I grew in strength, courage, and wisdom. No matter the storm, I stood firm because I knew He was with me, strengthening me with every step.

Through God's presence, my strength became unshakeable. He didn't just protect me from fear; He made me more powerful in every situation. With His help, I overcame every obstacle, and now I live with an unshakable confidence, knowing He is always by my side, giving me the strength to keep moving forward.

Testimony of Trusting God's Plan

There are times in life when we chase after things, and no matter how hard we try, we don't get what we hoped for. It can feel discouraging, and we might wonder why things aren't working out. But later, we often realize that what didn't happen was actually for our own good. In those moments, we understand that God's plan is far better than anything we could have imagined.

As the scripture says, *"And we know that in all things God works for the good of those who love him, who have been called according to his purpose."* (Romans 8:28). This verse reminds me that even when things don't go as we expect, God is still at work behind the scenes. Every circumstance, every setback, and every disappointment ultimately works together for our good.

There were times when I felt frustrated and disappointed because things didn't go my way. But as time passed, I realized that the things I thought I needed weren't actually what was best for me. God's timing, His plan, and His ways are always perfect, even when we can't see it in the moment.

Looking back, I can see how each closed door and each moment of waiting was part of God's greater plan to bring something better into my life. It wasn't a failure—it was a step toward the blessings He had in store for me. So, when things don't go as planned, trust that God is always working things out for your ultimate good. Every experience, every challenge, is shaping you for something greater.

Testimony of God's Faithfulness in Guiding My Path

God has always listened to me, always guided me to the right path, and opened doors when I needed them the most. Every step of the way, He has been there for me, leading me with His wisdom and grace. In every situation, whether big or small, I have seen His hand at work, directing me to the right choices and opening the way for me to succeed.

He has made my endeavors successful. I could never have accomplished what I did without His constant support. Every time I faced challenges, I saw how He opened new opportunities, provided the right solutions, and helped me move forward. His presence has been with me, reassuring me that I am never alone.

Whenever I faced moments of uncertainty, He was there to show me the way. His guidance has always been clear, and His timing perfect. I am so grateful for His unwavering faithfulness. He has truly made all my work successful and has been my constant companion through it all.

In every victory and every challenge, I can say with confidence that God has always been with me, showing me the way and making everything work out for my good.

Testimony of Faith and Surrender in Prayer

When we pray, we should do so with the firm belief that what we ask for will be given to us. Faith is the key—*believe* and you will *receive*. Once you pray and ask for something, do not worry about it anymore. Your lifestyle should be such that whenever you face worries or concerns, you simply remind yourself that what you've asked for has already been taken care of by God. It is no longer your responsibility; it's His.

Think about how Hannah prayed in the Bible—she prayed earnestly, and with complete surrender, she left everything in God's hands. When you pray, do so with the courage and confidence of a warrior, knowing that God will answer your prayers. After you pray, do not be afraid or worried. Just like a child comes to their father with all their needs, asking without hesitation or doubt, we must come to our Heavenly Father with the same trust. The child does not worry if the father has what they need, because they know that the father will provide.

We need to be like that child, trusting that our Heavenly Father has everything we need and that He will provide. Our job is not to worry about how, when, or in what form it will come. That's God's responsibility. Our job is simply to ask in faith and then live in confidence that He will answer. When you surrender everything, including your responsibilities, to God, He takes charge and works things out for you. Don't carry the burden of worry—just like a child trusts in their parent, trust in God with all your heart, knowing He is more than capable of providing what you need.

Believe in His ability to answer, and trust that He will always come through. Your part is to pray with faith, and then leave the rest to Him.

Testimony of Jesus' Sacrificial Love and God's Greater Plan

Jesus is the ocean of love, and His sacrifice on the cross is the greatest expression of that love. He gave His life for us in complete obedience to the will of His Father. Jesus' love for His Father was so deep that He did exactly what the Father asked, no matter how difficult or painful it was. The way He surrendered His will to God's plan teaches us how to walk in complete obedience and faith.

When we follow God's will, He leads us beyond our own understanding. God's plans for our lives are always greater than our own imaginations. We may think we know what's best for us, but God's purpose for us is far more magnificent than anything we can conceive. His plans are not limited by our thoughts—they are limitless, filled with hope, and aligned with His perfect will for us.

Just like Jesus perfectly fulfilled the Father's will, we are called to follow in His footsteps. When we align our desires with God's desires, He reveals a plan for our lives that far exceeds what we could ever expect. Sometimes, we may not understand the journey, but if we trust in God's greater purpose, we know that He is preparing us for something much bigger and more beautiful than we could ever dream. Jesus' life and sacrifice show us that obedience to God, even in the most difficult moments, opens the door to a greater future. His love never fails, and His plans for us are always good. If we walk in His will, we will see that His plan is not only bigger but also filled with blessings and a purpose that we could never have imagined.

Testimony of Faith Becoming Our Lifestyle

When faith truly becomes the foundation of our lives, it shapes every aspect of who we are. Faith is not just something we say or feel in our hearts, but it becomes the very way we live. It becomes a testimony of God's work in our lives, evident in everything we do. Our lifestyle, our behavior, our actions, and the way we respond to situations—all reflect the faith we have in God.

As believers, our walk with God should be reflected in our daily lives. The way we treat others, the way we handle challenges, and the way we carry ourselves all testify to the strength of our faith. Our lifestyle becomes a living testimony of God's grace and power. When we walk in faith, it shows in how we speak, how we act, and how we handle both the good and difficult times.

The Apostle James wrote that faith without works is dead (James 2:26). Our faith should be seen in our actions. When we trust God and walk according to His will, we become examples of His love and grace to others. Our life becomes a reflection of His truth, and people around us see the difference that faith makes.

Faith doesn't just change our hearts—it changes how we live. It transforms our mindset and our outlook on life. As we continue to grow in faith, our testimony becomes more evident. It's no longer just words we speak but the way we live that becomes a living witness to the power of God working in us.

Testimony: God's Faithfulness in Our Purchase

I want to share a testimony of God's amazing faithfulness and how He works in even the smallest details of our lives. My husband once needed to purchase an international software plugin, but there was a catch – the eligibility for the purchase was limited to a credit card from a specific bank. Unfortunately, we did not have an account with that bank, so it seemed impossible to proceed.

Despite the situation, my husband, with full faith, decided to try and make the purchase online, while praying and trusting God to work things out. We had no idea how it could work, but we believed that God could make a way.

To our surprise, when he entered the details and tried to pay, his debit card, which wasn't supposed to be eligible, was accepted. The transaction went through successfully, and we were able to make the purchase without any issues. It was truly a miracle that only God could have orchestrated.

This experience was a reminder that no matter how impossible a situation might seem, God is always in control. He can open doors and provide in ways we never expect. His faithfulness is beyond what we can imagine, and He cares about every detail of our lives—even something as small as an online purchase.

All the glory and praise be to God for making a way where there seemed to be no way.

Our Identity in Christ and the Power We Carry

As believers, our true identity is found in Christ. We are not just ordinary people; we are sons and daughters of the Most High God. The Bible tells us that we are made in God's image, and we carry the same power that Jesus carried when He walked on this earth. Jesus said, *"You will do greater works than I have done"* (John 14:12). Think about it—Jesus, who performed miracles, healed the sick, and cast out demons—has now passed that power and authority to us. It is up to us to recognize and walk in that authority.

Jesus gave us a command, and when He spoke, things happened immediately. In the same way, when we speak with faith, things should begin to happen. Our words, rooted in God's power, have the ability to move mountains. Jesus Himself said, *"If you have faith as small as a mustard seed, you can say to this mountain, 'Move from here to there,' and it will move"* (Matthew 17:20). This is the authority we have as believers in Christ.

We are called to live like Christ, to reflect His love, humility, and power. The Holy Spirit dwells in us, empowering us to carry out the work Jesus began on this earth. We are meant to be vessels of God's love, mercy, and kindness. Just as Jesus walked with compassion, healing, and delivering those in need, we are called to do the same.

Let us live with the understanding of the power and authority we carry in Christ. We are not powerless; we are filled with the same Holy Spirit that raised Jesus from the dead. Our identity in Christ should transform the way we live, speak, and act. When we recognize who we truly are, we step into the fullness of God's plan for our lives, walking in the love and power that Jesus demonstrated.

Be kind, humble, and full of love. Let the power of Christ flow through you in every situation. When we align our lives with God's will and walk in His authority, we will see lives changed, mountains moved, and the Kingdom of God advanced.

The Joy and Strength of a Believer

As believers, our faces should always reflect the joy and peace that come from knowing who we are in Christ. Sadness or despair should never define us because we are children of the living God, the Creator of the entire universe. Our Father is the one who holds all things in His hands, and when He is with us, there is no reason for us to be sad or downcast.

When difficulties or worries arise, we should remember that we have the authority to overcome them. These challenges are simply distractions, things that try to pull us away from our true purpose and the path God has set for us. We must not allow these distractions to steal our joy, peace, or faith. Instead, we have the power to rebuke them in Jesus' name, knowing that nothing can separate us from God's love and His plans for us.

Our relationship with God is the most important thing, and nothing can come between us and Him. No situation, no trial, no external circumstance should ever cause us to lose sight of His presence and the victory He has already won for us. As His children, we are called to walk in His joy, strength, and peace, no matter the circumstances.

The Bible tells us that the joy of the Lord is our strength (Nehemiah 8:10). When we focus on God's goodness, His promises, and His faithfulness, we can remain strong and unwavering, no matter what comes our way. So, when worries or doubts try to creep in, recognize them for what they are—temporary distractions—and declare God's truth over your life. Keep your focus on Him, and let His joy be evident in every part of your life.

The Truth Over Lies: God's Truth is Our Reality

Difficulties, pain, failure, and rejection are all lies that the enemy tries to use to shake our faith. These things may seem real in the moment, but they are not our truth. The only truth we need to hold onto is the Word of God. God's truth is eternal and unchanging.

The Bible tells us that in this world, we will face troubles, but we should take heart because Jesus has overcome the world (John 16:33). These challenges are temporary, and they do not define who we are. Our identity is not based on our circumstances, but on the truth of who we are in Christ. We are more than conquerors through Him who loves us (Romans 8:37).

Pain and failure are only temporary, and rejection does not define our worth. The Creator of the universe loves us, and He has a plan for our lives that is greater than anything we can imagine. His truth tells us that we are fearfully and wonderfully made (Psalm 139:14), and that He will never leave us nor forsake us (Deuteronomy 31:6).

When we focus on God's truth, we see our lives through His eyes. His promises are yes and amen (2 Corinthians 1:20). We are victorious because of what Jesus has done for us. No matter what we face, we have the victory in Him, and nothing can separate us from His love.

So, let go of the lies that try to hold you down—whether it's pain, rejection, failure, or doubt. Embrace the truth of God's Word, because that is the only truth that matters. He is the way, the truth, and the life (John 14:6), and in Him, we have everything we need to overcome.

God's Promises Are Sure and True

God's promises are not just words—they are truths that we can stand on with unwavering faith. The verse you mentioned reflects God's assurance of provision, care, and faithfulness in our lives. *"The Lord is my shepherd; I shall not want"* (Psalm 23:1). This powerful promise reminds us that when we trust in Him, we will lack nothing good. Our needs, whether physical, emotional, or spiritual, will be met because God is faithful to fulfill every promise He has made.

God is not like man who may break promises or fail to deliver. He is the eternal, unchanging, and all-powerful Creator who never fails to keep His word. As Numbers 23:19 says, *"God is not a man that He should lie, nor a son of man that He should change His mind. Does He speak and then not act? Does He promise and not fulfill?"* God is the ultimate promise keeper, and His words are powerful and true.

When we put our trust in Him, He provides abundantly for us. *"And my God will meet all your needs according to the riches of his glory in Christ Jesus"* (Philippians 4:19). This means that we will never lack what is necessary for us. His promises of provision, peace, protection, and strength are guaranteed. We do not have to worry or fear because God is committed to fulfilling His word.

No matter what the world may say or what challenges we may face, remember that God's promises are alive and powerful. His word will not return void (Isaiah 55:11), and

He will always make sure that we are cared for. Keep your faith anchored in His promises, and you will never be empty or lacking—He is the source of all that is good.

Believe in His word, trust in His timing, and live with the assurance that He is always with you, providing and fulfilling His promises in your life.

Strength in Our Weakness

In our moments of weakness, God's strength is made perfect. The Bible teaches us that when we feel weak, that is when God's power shines through the most. *"But he said to me, 'My grace is sufficient for you, for my power is made perfect in weakness.'"* (2 Corinthians 12:9). This is such a beautiful reminder that our limitations don't define us, but God's presence in our lives does.

When we are at our lowest, that is often when we feel God's nearness the most. In the midst of brokenness, He is there to heal, comfort, and strengthen us. *"The Lord is close to the brokenhearted and saves those who are crushed in spirit."* (Psalm 34:18). It is in our moments of vulnerability and pain that God's love and presence are closest to us, lifting us up and giving us strength beyond what we can imagine.

When our hearts are shattered and we feel defeated, God's grace fills the gaps and transforms our weakness into a source of strength. He doesn't leave us in our struggles; rather, He draws near to us, embracing us with His love and providing the strength we need to keep going.

So, when you feel weak or overwhelmed, remember that God is right there with you, offering His strength. Your weakness does not make you less; it makes space for God's power to work in you and through you. With Him, you can overcome anything. Trust that He is near, and in your weakness, He will give you the strength to rise again.

Light of the World

In this world, we are called to be the light. The Bible reminds us, *"You are the light of the world."* We are the children of light, shining bright like the sun. Just like the sun radiates its light and warmth, we too must glow with the power of Christ, carrying His brilliance into every dark corner of the world.

We are not meant to remain dimmed, hidden away in shadows. The darkness of this world can never overpower us because the light of God is within us. *"The light shines in the darkness, and the darkness has not overcome it."* (John 1:5)

Authority in Christ

We are chosen, we are royalty, and we are heirs of the kingdom. God created us to reign, to rule over darkness, to stand firm in His power. As children of the Most High, we carry His authority and have dominion over the powers of evil. No force of darkness can harm us. They flee when we stand firm in Christ because they have no authority over us. We are the generation that carries God's power—His authority flows through us. Whether it's the storms of life, trials, or temptations, we remain unshaken because we have been made to rule. Our existence is marked by victory. We are called not only to endure but to conquer, to rise above, to shine in every circumstance.

Light Prevails Over Darkness

Darkness has no lasting hold over us. We are born of the light, and the light reigns in our lives. When we stand in the power of Christ, the shadows cannot exist in the same space. They must flee. The rulers of this world tremble before the authority we carry. Nothing can touch us unless we allow it, because we are protected by the power of God. No hardship can weigh us down. Our circumstances cannot hold us captive because we are a chosen people, a royal priesthood. As children of light, we carry the power to break chains, to set captives free, and to shine brighter every day. No matter what, we know that victory is ours through Christ, who strengthens us.

Walking in God's Authority

In Christ, we have been empowered to speak with authority. We don't need to be passive when challenges come. We have the authority to rebuke every attack, to command peace, and to declare victory. With Christ in us, we become agents of change, dismantling the works of darkness wherever we go.

In Christ, we are unstoppable. Nothing can stand against us, and we don't shy away from confronting evil. We take authority over every situation. Whether it's sickness, fear, or doubt, we speak the name of Jesus, and darkness must bow down.

Living as Overcomers

We are not meant to live as victims. We have been called to be victors, to overcome, and to shine. Christ's victory over sin, death, and darkness is our victory. We live boldly because the power of Christ works in us, giving us the strength to face anything. Our identity is grounded in His love, and we will never be defeated.

Our lives should be a reflection of the power of Christ. We live with authority, knowing that we have the power to change the atmosphere, to bring light into darkness, and to declare God's kingdom on Earth. We are meant to walk in power, shine with glory, and rule with Christ forever.

In Him, we are more than conquerors.

Cleaning the Inner House

Just as we clean our homes and remove all the garbage, we must also cleanse our minds. Every negative thought, every harmful idea, and every destructive plan that tries to settle in our hearts must be cast out. Imagine your mind as a house—just as you wouldn't allow trash to pile up in your living space, don't let negative or harmful thoughts take up residence in your mind.

When negative thoughts knock at the door of your mind, don't open it. Don't give them permission to enter. Just like you wouldn't invite a stranger into your home, don't welcome thoughts that do not align with God's truth. The world may try to offer you its version of reality, but the true reality is what the Spirit of God reveals to you. The world's perspective is often based on appearances, but the truth of God, as guided by the Holy Spirit, always leads you towards righteousness and peace.

Every time a negative thought arises, immediately reject it. Don't accept it as part of your story. Focus on what is true, pure, noble, and of good report—those are the thoughts that should fill your mind. Remember, *"Whatever is true, whatever is noble, whatever is right, whatever is pure, whatever is lovely, and whatever is admirable— if anything is excellent or praiseworthy — think about such things."* (Philippians 4:8)

Embracing God's Truth

When you make space in your heart for God's truth, it will guide you. The world may offer false promises, but only God can lead you to peace and purpose. Let your mind be filled with His Word. Every time a lie or a false thought knocks on your door, open it to God's truth. Let Him cleanse you from within. Allow the Holy Spirit to help you discern what is of God and what is of the world.

Don't let the chaos of the world influence you. Your thoughts are precious, and you have the power to choose which ones you embrace. Reject the lies, reject the doubts, and stand firm in the truth of God. He has created you to live in His light, to walk in His ways, and to follow the path that leads to peace and joy.

The Mind of Christ

When we reject the world's lies, we make space for the mind of Christ to shape our thoughts. The Holy Spirit renews our minds and transforms us into the image of Christ. As we align our thoughts with His Word, we begin to think like Him, speak like Him, and act like Him.

This transformation is not an overnight process, but as we continue to seek God and meditate on His Word, we become more and more like Christ. We begin to see things through His eyes and understand the world from His perspective. The lies of the world lose their grip on us, and we are free to live the life God has called us to live.

Guarding Your Heart and Mind

It is essential to guard your heart and mind from negativity. Be vigilant about what you allow to enter your thoughts. Just as a home can become cluttered with garbage, your mind can become cluttered with negative thoughts if you are not careful. Guard your thoughts by filling your mind with the Word of God and the truth of who you are in Christ.

When you focus on God's Word, you begin to see life through His lens. You realize that you are more than a conqueror, that you are loved, and that you are destined for great things. Don't let the world's lies distract you. Instead, focus on what God has spoken over your life, and let His truth lead you to peace and fulfillment.

Leaving Judgment to God

In this world, we often encounter situations where others wrong us, or where we feel someone is acting unjustly. But in those moments, we must remember: it is not our place to judge others. God has not called us to condemn, but to love. When we see someone acting in a way that seems wrong, it is not our responsibility to pass judgment on them. We are not called to correct others with harshness or to call them out publicly, but to show compassion and leave judgment in the hands of God.

When someone wrongs you, don't hold on to bitterness or anger. Instead, release them into God's hands, and trust that He will deal with the situation in His time and way. It's easy to feel the urge to get even, to speak harshly, or to retaliate, but that only keeps us trapped in negativity.

Instead, let your words be filled with blessings, not curses. Let your heart remain pure and full of love.

"Do not repay anyone evil for evil... If it is possible, as far as it depends on you, live at peace with everyone." (Romans 12:17-18)

When someone wrongs us, we don't retaliate, we don't allow our hearts to become hardened. We give it to God and trust that He will handle it with perfect justice. In the meantime, we pray for those who have hurt us and let our actions reflect God's love, not the anger we might feel.

Our behavior should always be gentle, kind, and humble. Humility is key—never allow pride to enter your heart. God wants us to live in peace, to show gratitude for all things, and to remain joyful even when things are difficult. *"Give thanks in all circumstances; for this is God's will for you in Christ Jesus."* (1 Thessalonians 5:18)

Even when things seem unfair, we don't complain or grumble. Instead, we choose to see the hand of God in every situation. Gratitude transforms our hearts and brings peace.

A Sweet and Gentle Spirit

Our demeanor should always be gentle and kind. Whether we are facing a disagreement or a difficult situation, our words should be full of grace. When you speak, let your words be filled with kindness, even when correcting someone. Our behavior should always reflect Christ—compassionate, understanding, and forgiving.

There is no place for arrogance or pride in a believer's life. Instead, we are called to humility, always remembering that every blessing we have comes from God. There is no room for boasting or a sense of superiority. In everything, give thanks to God, for He has been good to us and has given us all we need to live a peaceful and joyful life.

When we allow pride to creep in, it damages our relationships and steals our joy. But when we remain humble, grateful, and full of love, we become a reflection of God's character to the world.

Trusting God's Timing

Sometimes, life feels unfair. People might treat us poorly, and situations may seem unjust. But we must trust that God's timing is perfect. He sees all, and He will right every wrong in His way. Our role is not to take matters into our own hands, but to trust that God is in control and that He will bring justice in His time.

When we focus on gratitude and humility, we shift our focus from the wrongs done to us to the goodness of God. We begin to see His hand in every situation and know that He is working all things for our good.

Instead of growing bitter or angry, let's choose peace. Let's choose to release every negative thought, every judgment, and every grudge. Let's make space for God's love and forgiveness to flow through us. And when others wrong us, let's bless them with our words and pray for them, trusting that God will do the rest.

Begin Every Work with God's Name

Every task we undertake, no matter how big or small, should be started with the name of the Lord. In everything we do, we must acknowledge that it is through God's grace and guidance that we are able to accomplish anything. Before you begin any work, whether it's a simple household chore, your professional duties, or a personal project, start by calling on the name of the Lord.

"Whatever you do, do it all for the glory of God." (1 Corinthians 10:31)

This verse reminds us that every action, no matter how ordinary, has the potential to bring glory to God when done with the right heart. Before you start, say with faith: *"Lord, I dedicate this work to You. I invite Your presence to guide me through it. I declare that You are with me, and I trust You to bless and multiply my efforts."*

Never approach your tasks with complaints or negative thoughts. *"Do all things without grumbling or disputing."* (Philippians 2:14) The way we approach our work matters. If we approach it with a heart of gratitude, with a mindset that this task is an opportunity to serve God, we will find joy in it. Complaining or speaking negatively only invites frustration and failure, but when we speak with faith and gratitude, we open the door to God's blessing.

Start every endeavor with this declaration:

"Lord, I thank You for the ability to do this work. I know that it is through Your grace that I am able to accomplish anything. Thank You for blessing my efforts. I declare that

You have opened the path for success and that You will lead me every step of the way."

By declaring your work as blessed by God, you are setting the tone for success. You are inviting God to take control of the process, to make it fruitful, and to guide you with wisdom. Success is not always measured by visible results, but by the peace and confidence you experience knowing that God is in control.

Even when challenges arise, remember that God is with you. Keep your attitude positive and your faith strong. Instead of focusing on the obstacles, focus on God's promises. He will provide the strength and resources needed to overcome any difficulty.

Walking in God's Blessing

As you continue to declare God's blessing over your work, you will begin to see His hand moving in powerful ways. When we acknowledge God in all that we do, we open ourselves to His provision and guidance.

When you feel tired or frustrated, remind yourself that God has already blessed your efforts. Say, *"Lord, I trust You. I know that You are working through me, and I receive Your grace and strength to complete this task successfully."*

By starting each task with God's name and giving thanks before you even begin, you are demonstrating your trust in His plans for you. You are not relying on your own strength or wisdom, but on His unlimited power to make your efforts fruitful. God's favor goes before you, and He will open doors of opportunity that you could never have opened on your own.

Let God Be the Source of Your Success

Success is not the result of our own abilities or hard work alone, but it is the favor of God that empowers us to succeed. It is He who makes the path straight, who gives us the wisdom and creativity to solve problems, and who provides the resources we need.

So, before you begin any task, always thank God for His guidance. Declare His blessings over every step you take, and trust that He will make your efforts prosper. Whether you succeed or face difficulties, you can rest in the assurance that God is in control.

Trust in God's Provision

Remember, every task is an opportunity to trust God more. Keep Him at the center of your work, and let His peace guard your heart. When you do this, not only will you see success in your work, but you will also grow closer to Him. Whether you are working for yourself, for others, or for the glory of God, make sure to do it with a heart full of gratitude and faith.

God's Unfailing Provision

I want to share how wonderfully God has worked in my life, showing me that He never lets anyone's hope be shattered. Every time I have had a need or a desire, God has always provided, often in ways I never expected. His ways are beyond my understanding, and His timing is perfect.

There have been moments when I thought I was asking for something specific, but God, in His infinite wisdom, gave me something even better. I realized that His plans for me are far greater than anything I could have imagined. Where

I saw a limitation, He saw opportunity, and where I had doubts, He poured His blessings over me in abundance.

God's provision is always abundant, always good, and always on time. I have learned that when we trust Him completely, He never fails to meet our needs—and often He gives us more than what we had hoped for.

His love and faithfulness are unshakable. Whatever I needed, He provided, and what I received was always better than what I initially asked for. God's promises are true, and He is always faithful to His word.

To Him be all the glory for His abundant grace and provision!

My Journey of Faith and God's Faithfulness

When I look back at my life, I see how God has been with me through every twist and turn, guiding me, providing for me, and strengthening my faith. It all started when God chose me and established a deeper connection with Him after my marriage. Before I got married, my relationship with God was already strong, but after the wedding, things changed in a way I never expected.

Before my marriage, I used to attend prayer meetings once in a while, and I felt God's presence in those moments. My direct connection with God was real, and He was always there to support me, to guide me. I always felt His hand upon me, but little did I know that after my marriage, my faith would be tested in ways I never anticipated.

Before my marriage, I was working professionally, and I didn't have much time for household responsibilities. Cooking wasn't something I knew how to do; it wasn't something I had the interest or the time for because of my demanding career. After I resigned from my job, I was eager to join a new company, but just a few days after my marriage, I learned that the company I was about to join had been taken over by someone else. It felt like a setback, and I couldn't understand why things were turning out this way.

At home, things were even more difficult. The servant who used to help us around the house was removed by my in-laws, and I found myself in a strange situation. There were customs and traditions that my in-laws followed, but they didn't align with my beliefs. I couldn't accept practices like bowing down to idols or following rituals that went against my loyalty to God. My heart was firmly rooted in my relationship with the Lord, and I couldn't compromise that. Things started to become tense. My husband, however, began to grow in his faith, sitting down to pray and choosing to reject the worship of idols as well. He too made the decision not to bow to any other gods. This caused conflict in our home, and one day, in the midst of all the tension, my in-laws told us to leave. They told us to pack up and leave the house. The language they used was harsh, and even my sisters-in-law and their husbands joined in on the phone calls, criticizing us. I cried a lot that day, but I knew that through it all, my hope in God through Jesus was bigger than any problem I faced.

In that difficult moment, my husband and I turned to God in prayer. We sat together and sought His guidance. And that's when God spoke to us through His Word. He reminded us of the verse, *"Do not let your heart be troubled. In my Father's house are many rooms. If it were not so, I would have told you."* (John 14:2). These words gave us peace and comfort when we felt lost. As we stood on the terrace looking at the stars, we prayed and talked to God, trusting in His promises.

God spoke to our hearts and reassured us: *"I have prepared a place for you. I have prepared work for you. I have prepared earnings for you. Everything will be alright."* In that moment, we packed our things with God's guidance and left our home on the morning of August 6, 2023, at 4

AM. We left everything behind, trusting God's plan for us. We stayed with someone for a few days, but we knew that God had something greater in store for us.

Just as we had written down, *"We have received our new home and business in 2023,"* God made it happen. He provided us with a new home, and my husband's company began to flourish in a way we had never imagined. Everything started to fall into place.

The lesson I learned through this journey is simple: Remember the promises God has made to you. His promises are true. He doesn't change, and He will always be with you. His Word is steadfast, and He will never leave you nor forsake you. I've seen it in my own life—how God works in unexpected ways, opening doors and providing exactly what you need, even when things seem uncertain. God's promises are unchanging, and when you trust Him, He will lead you, guide you, and provide for you in every area of your life. Through it all, I've learned to hold on to His promises and trust that He is faithful, no matter the circumstances. He is always with you, and His plans for you are good.

We Live By Faith Not By sight

The Bible teaches us in **2 Corinthians 5:7**, "For we walk by faith, not by sight." This scripture reveals a profound truth: we are not called to live based on what we see with our natural eyes, but based on what we know to be true in our hearts through our relationship with Christ. In our world, it is so easy to be swayed by what we see around us, by our circumstances, or by the limitations that seem to be placed before us. But as believers, we are called to a higher standard—a life of unwavering faith.

The Decision to Believe

When you choose to believe in God, you're making a decision to trust in His promises, to rely on His guidance, and to have confidence in His provision. This faith doesn't simply mean hoping for the best or wishing for good things to happen; it means being fully persuaded in your heart that God will fulfill His promises and that everything He says is true. It means trusting in His Word even when the evidence seems contrary.

In the book of **Mark 11:24**, Jesus teaches us, "Therefore I tell you, whatever you ask for in prayer, believe that you have received it, and it will be yours." This isn't just a suggestion, but a command. It challenges us to believe beyond the visible, to trust in God's ability to bring about what we ask, even before we see it. This is the essence of living by faith—trusting in God's promises and acting upon them, knowing that He is faithful to perform what He has said.

The Faith That Moves Mountains

Faith in Christ allows us to move beyond the limitations of the natural world. In **Matthew 17:20**, Jesus says, "If you have faith as small as a mustard seed, you can say to this mountain, 'Move from here to there,' and it will move. Nothing will be impossible for you." This passage reveals the enormous power that faith holds. A small amount of faith in Christ is all it takes to achieve the impossible, because it's not the size of our faith that matters, but the power of the God we place our faith in.

When we face challenges in life, it may seem as though we're standing before an insurmountable mountain. But faith allows us to speak to that mountain and command it to move. It's not about relying on our own strength or abilities, but about trusting that God can do what we cannot. We live by faith, not by sight, because the mountains in our lives are not obstacles to God—they are opportunities for His power to be displayed.

Faith in Action: Trusting God's Timing

Faith also means trusting God's timing. Too often, we want immediate results, but God's timing is always perfect. Our understanding is limited, but God sees the bigger picture. What seems delayed to us is often an opportunity for God to work behind the scenes, preparing the way for something greater. When we trust in God's perfect timing, we can rest assured that He is working things out for our good.

Take the example of **Abraham**. In the book of **Genesis**, God promised Abraham that he would be the father of many nations. But it took years for this promise to be fulfilled. Abraham's faith was tested over and over again, and at times, he doubted. Yet, through it all, he continued to believe in God's promise. In the end, God's timing was perfect, and Abraham became the father of a great nation. Abraham's story reminds us that while we may not see the results immediately, faith assures us that God's promises are never delayed—they are always right on time.

A Life of Unwavering Belief

So, what does it look like to live by faith through Christ? It means fully trusting in God for everything—our needs, our dreams, our goals, and even our challenges. It means trusting that He is working on our behalf even when we don't see immediate results. It means being determined in our hearts that no matter what happens, we will continue to believe in God's goodness, His power, and His provision. This unwavering belief is not just for big moments, like purchasing a home or achieving a career goal. It's for every aspect of life—every day, every decision, every step we take. When we believe in God through Christ, we are not living passively. We are actively walking in the assurance that God is with us, leading us, and enabling us to do all things through Christ who strengthens us.

In **Philippians 4:13**, Paul reminds us, "I can do all things through Christ who strengthens me." This isn't just a hopeful statement; it's a declaration of faith. Christ's strength empowers us to overcome every challenge and achieve every goal that is aligned with His will. Our faith in

Him gives us the courage to step out, even when the path ahead is uncertain.

Sometimes God Calls Us to Stay Away from Certain People

There are moments in our lives when God calls us to maintain distance from certain individuals. We may not always understand the reason at first, but it is important to trust His guidance. Many times, people around us fail to understand our love and intentions. Instead of appreciating it, they take advantage of us. But the Lord, in His wisdom, guides us on how to walk through such challenges.

As we continue to grow in our walk with Jesus Christ, we begin to notice that some people, who were once close to us, start drifting away. This isn't by accident. As we step deeper into the life of Christ, we begin to shed the impurities of the world, and we no longer attract or align with those whose actions are guided by deceit, lies, and selfishness. Those who live in manipulation and dishonesty will often distance themselves from us as our paths diverge. God protects us in these situations. He shields us from the deceit and trickery of others, guiding us to make decisions that are in line with His will. He knows what is best for us and is always working behind the scenes to safeguard our hearts, our minds, and our futures. What may seem like a loss of relationships is actually a divine protection, removing the negative influences that could have hurt us in the long run.

As we grow in Christ, we must be prepared to let go of those who do not share in the same values or intentions.

This does not mean we are to stop loving them or praying for them, but we must recognize that sometimes God removes people from our lives to shield us from harm, to keep us focused on Him, and to protect our spiritual journey.

Let us trust that God's plan is always better than our own understanding. He knows the hearts of all people and will guide us toward those who will help us grow, while gently distancing us from those who may cause us to stumble. Through His grace, we are protected from the schemes of others, and we are led toward His perfect will.

The Battle is Not Yours

Psalm 118:14 declares, *"The Lord is my strength and my song; He has become my salvation."* When God has chosen you, when He has set you apart, the battles you face are not yours to fight alone. They belong to Him. This truth is so powerful—it's not about your strength or ability, but about God's power and His plan for your life.

In life, there will be moments when everything feels overwhelming, when the weight of the world is on your shoulders. During those times, it's easy to feel like giving up, to feel like you can't go any further. But God's word tells us—*do not give up*. You were never meant to fight these battles by yourself. When you feel down, when you feel discouraged, remember that the victory is already secured by the Lord.

No matter the situation, no matter how difficult it gets, *never* let frustration control you. Don't let it come out of your mouth, don't let it define you. Words are powerful, and they shape our reality. Speak life, speak faith, even when everything around you seems bleak. The Lord is with you, and He is your strength.

Sometimes, we can be tempted to say things about ourselves that are not in line with who God says we are. We may speak negativity over our own lives, doubting ourselves, thinking we are incapable or unworthy. But this is not the truth. Remember, God has a purpose for you, and He is the one fighting for you. Don't speak against the greatness God has placed inside you. Speak His promises over your life, because His power is greater than anything you are facing.

Whatever the battle may be—whether it's in your relationships, your job, your health, or your future—know that *the battle is not yours*. It belongs to God. He has already gone before you, and He will see you through. Trust Him. Keep your faith in Him. God can do the impossible.

As you walk through every challenge, don't forget this truth: *The battle is His.* You are His child, and He is on your side, guiding you, strengthening you, and fighting for you. Never lose hope, never give up, and never let the lies of defeat speak louder than the victory that is already yours in Christ.

Faith like Joshua's - Believe to Receive

Our faith should be strong, unwavering, and fully placed in God. The kind of faith that Joshua had in the Lord is truly inspiring. Joshua's faith was so impactful that it led to the miraculous falling of the walls of Jericho. When God commanded Joshua to walk around the walls of Jericho for seven days and on the seventh day shout with praise, Joshua did exactly as God instructed. There was no doubt, no hesitation—he followed God's word with complete faith.

For six days, Joshua and the people of Israel marched around the city without seeing any visible result. But on the seventh day, after praising and thanking God, the walls came down. Why? Because Joshua believed in the promise of God. He trusted that what God said would happen, no matter how impossible it seemed. Joshua didn't question, he didn't falter, he simply trusted.

This is the kind of faith we are called to have. Just as God told Joshua to act with faith, we are made in His image and have been given the same authority. We, too, are called to speak with faith and authority. When we declare something in the name of Jesus, it will be done—if we speak with belief and confidence in the power of God.

We have the authority given by God Himself, and with that authority comes the responsibility to believe. When we speak in faith, we need to truly believe that what we are asking for will come to pass. Whatever we ask in His name, we will receive, but we must believe with unwavering faith. Just like the walls of Jericho came down, the obstacles in our lives can also be broken when we trust God completely. Whatever the walls may be in your life—whether it's fear, doubt, sickness, or any other challenge—remember that if you believe and trust in God, those walls will fall. The key is believing with faith and authority.

When we come before God, we must ask with faith, knowing that He will provide. Whatever you ask for in prayer, believe that you will receive it, and continually thank God for what is to come. Faith is not just about asking; it's about trusting and giving thanks even before we see the results.

Believe that when you pray, what you are asking for will come to pass. Believe in God's promises and walk in faith. Just as the walls of Jericho fell when Joshua trusted and obeyed, the obstacles in your life will also be overcome through faith and trust in the Lord. Your faith will break down every barrier, and with gratitude, you will witness the power of God's promises in your life.

Believe to Receive – Faith in Jesus

Belief is not just a word; it's a powerful force that unlocks everything we need in life. Many people talk about faith, but how many actually live it? True faith is not about hesitation, doubt, or fear—it's about a bold, unwavering trust in Jesus' promises.

When you believe in Jesus, you believe in the source of all provision. In His name, you receive everything you need. It's not about begging or pleading; it's about knowing that what you ask for is already yours. Faith isn't asking in doubt—it's receiving with thanksgiving. Thanking God that everything you need is already on its way.

One of the biggest mistakes many people make is letting fear or hesitation stop them from fully walking in faith. When you truly believe, fear has no place. There is no room for second-guessing, no space for holding back. You must speak boldly, and expect that your needs will be met. You are a child of God, and He promises to provide. So why hesitate? Why doubt?

But belief is not just about words—it's about action. Faith in Jesus should affect every part of your life. It should shape how you think, what you say, and what you do. If you believe that Jesus will provide, then start living as though you already have what you've asked for. Faith is not just a thought; it's a lifestyle. When you truly believe, it changes the way you carry yourself, the way you speak, and the way you act.

I've experienced this in my own life. I don't beg or plead for anything. I don't ask in doubt. I simply thank God because I know that what I need is already coming to me. When I pray in Jesus' name, I expect results. I believe in His power to deliver, and I walk in the confidence that I will receive. This is how faith works—it's not just about asking, it's about knowing and trusting that God will answer.

Once you believe, don't let anything or anyone shake your faith. You must remain determined. The world might try to get you to doubt, your circumstances might challenge you, but hold on to your faith. Keep speaking your needs with boldness, keep thanking God, and keep walking in confidence. Your faith will open doors, bring blessings, and transform your life.

To receive, you must first believe. It's as simple as that. Believe in Jesus' power to provide for you, speak your needs with boldness, and live your faith out loud. When you do, you will receive everything you need and more. God is faithful to His word—what you believe, you will receive. So stand strong, speak your faith, and watch God work in your life.

The Power of Diligence and Faith

"Lazy hands make a man poor, but diligent hands bring wealth. The blessing of the Lord brings wealth, and He adds no trouble to it."

- **Proverbs 10:4, 22**

Success, prosperity, and wealth in life are not just a result of hard work; they are also tied to the right direction and God's blessing. If you are lazy or neglect your responsibilities, the outcomes will inevitably be unfavorable. However, those who approach their work with honesty, diligence, and commitment are the ones who find stability and prosperity in life.

When you do your work with full integrity and dedication, you will not be afraid of any challenges. You understand that the reward for hard work is always sweet, even if the results don't come immediately. This principle applies not only in the material world but also in the spiritual realm.

Never forget that "faith without works is dead, and works without faith are incomplete." If we only believe but do not work, our faith is incomplete. Likewise, if we only work without faith, our efforts lack purpose. Both must go hand in hand for true success.

Proverbs tells us that wealth comes from "the blessing of the Lord," and this blessing does not bring sorrow with it. This is clear: the source of true success and prosperity is not just our hard work, but also God's blessing. When we work with honesty and maintain faith in God, He blesses us with what we need. His blessings bring peace, contentment, and prosperity without adding any sorrow or burden.

The most important thing in life is to approach our work with integrity and diligence, while also keeping our faith in God, knowing that He will guide and bless us every step of the way. He will never let us fail, and He will never allow our efforts to go to waste. With the combined strength of both hard work and faith, we can move our lives toward growth and success.

The Power of Walking in the Word

One day, we had a Prayer meeting at our home, and during the session, one of the attendees shared something that caught my attention. He said, "When I speak God's word to others, I speak with great courage and confidence. But when it comes to applying those words to my own life, I don't always live by them the same way. I find myself struggling to walk in faith when the situation is mine."

This statement made me reflect deeply on how many of us, including myself at times, can boldly speak God's word to others but hesitate when it comes to applying it to our own lives. It is easy to encourage others with faith and scripture, but when the test comes, we often falter. So, I thought about how to answer him, and I turned to God's word for the solution.

I responded, "It's not enough to just hear the word or even speak it. You must *live* it. We are called to be not just hearers of the word, but doers of it. The challenge is not merely in listening to the word, but in walking in it. Just speaking God's promises isn't enough. We must surrender our hearts and minds completely to Him."

I shared with him that surrendering to God is not a one-time act but a daily commitment. Every moment, we must turn our minds toward Him. I told him, "Always remember, your mind should be loyal and faithful to God. Never say, 'My mind is restless' or 'I can't control my thoughts.'

Instead, speak life over your mind and thoughts. Speak, 'My mind is loyal to God, and it will follow His word.'"

I explained that it's not just about saying the right things, but about walking in the truth of those words. We need to be consistently aligned with God's word and live it out. God's word is sharp, like a double-edged sword, and it has the power to change situations. The word of God is alive, and when we truly walk in it, it transforms our lives.

It is crucial to stay connected to God's word. Listening to it is good, but applying it is where the power lies. We need to be steadfast in His word and consistently walk according to His truth, no matter the circumstances. This means, even when challenges come, we must remind ourselves to hold onto God's promises and let them guide our actions.

The most important thing is to always keep our minds focused on God. When we face struggles, it's easy to get distracted by fear or doubt, but if we keep our hearts and minds surrendered to Him, we will find the strength to overcome any situation. I encouraged him, and everyone present, to always speak life over their minds. No matter how tough things may seem, we must always say, "I am loyal to God's word, and I trust in His strength."

In the end, I reminded them: "It's not enough to hear the word, and it's not enough to speak the word. We must live the word. Walking in God's word every day is what gives us the power to endure, to overcome, and to be transformed."

The Unchanging Blessings of God

"Every good and perfect gift is from above, coming down from the Father of the heavenly lights, who does not change like shifting shadows."

— James 1:17

In life, we often seek blessings, whether in the form of peace, provision, health, or relationships. We pray, we strive, and we hope for these blessings to come into our lives. But there is one truth that remains constant: all good gifts come from God, and He does not change. The blessings that come from God are unshakable, dependable, and eternal.

God is described as the "Father of the heavenly lights," meaning He is the Creator of everything, and in His nature, He is constant. Unlike the world around us, which is filled with uncertainty, change, and sometimes confusion, God's blessings remain steady and unchanging. The verse reminds us that there is no "variation or shadow of turning" with Him. This means that God's promises and gifts are reliable; they do not fluctuate with circumstances or seasons.

Think about it: everything good that we experience in life—whether it is a moment of joy, a breakthrough, or a provision in times of need—is a gift from God. But unlike worldly possessions, which can break, fade, or be lost, God's blessings are eternal. They are founded in His love, and He will never take them away from us. He is the giver of good gifts, and these gifts reflect His unwavering character.

This truth is a powerful reminder for us to trust in God's constancy. Life may bring challenges, and sometimes we may feel as if things are changing or falling apart. However, we can be certain that God's love for us does not change. His promises are true and remain firm, no matter what we face.

When we feel uncertain or discouraged, we can look to God, who is unchanging, and know that His blessings are still flowing toward us. Just as the sun remains constant in the sky, bringing light and warmth every day, God's blessings remain consistent, filling our lives with the goodness and grace we need to endure.

God's faithfulness is not dependent on our performance or the situation around us. It is based on His nature, which is perfect, unchanging, and eternal. This is a source of great comfort, because we can always count on God's goodness, regardless of the ups and downs of life.

When life feels uncertain, remember that every good gift in your life has come from God. His blessings are not temporary or fleeting; they are eternal. God doesn't change like the shadows cast by the sun; He remains the same yesterday, today, and forever. Trust in His unchanging nature and know that the blessings He gives you will never fade or be taken away. They are a reflection of His love, and He will always provide for you in every season of life.

Created for His Glory

"He chose to give us birth through the word of truth, that we might be a kind of firstfruits of all he created."
— **James 1:18**

We are the highest and most precious creation of God. Each of us is formed by His hands, and our lives are meant to bring Him glory and praise. God, in His infinite wisdom and love, created us with a specific purpose: to reflect His goodness, to honor His greatness, and to live in a way that magnifies Him. The very fact that we exist, that we are living and breathing, is a testament to His greatness.

Our lives are not a result of random chance or mere circumstance. We are created by the will of the most powerful and most excellent Creator. The Bible tells us that God, by His own desire, gave us life through His truth. This truth is His word, and it is through His word that we are born into a new life—an eternal life that has meaning, purpose, and value.

As His creation, we are called to be the "firstfruits" among His creatures. Just as the first fruits of a harvest are the best and most prized portion, we are called to live in a way that reflects God's beauty and goodness. Our lives should bear witness to the Creator's love and grace. We are His workmanship, created to be a living testimony of His truth and glory.

God's creation is perfect, and we, as His most precious creation, are called to live in alignment with that perfection. Our lives are not meant to be consumed with pointless worries or fleeting desires. The things of this world, the material possessions, the fame, and the success, are temporary. These things will pass away, and they will not satisfy the deepest longings of our hearts.

We are reminded that we don't need to chase after the fleeting pleasures of this world. God has already provided us with everything we need for life and godliness. There is no need to run after the empty pursuits that the world offers. Instead, we are to seek after God, to dwell in His presence, and to fulfill His purpose for us.

The truth is, we have already conquered this world in Christ. The victory is won. We are not to be anxious or fearful about the things of this world. We are called to reign with Christ, not to chase after the things that will fade away. We have been given dominion over this world, not to be ruled by it. Our focus should be on His kingdom, His will, and His purpose.

In Christ, we have already achieved the victory. We are no longer bound by the desires and pressures of the world. Instead, we are called to live as citizens of Heaven, with a higher purpose. Our purpose is to glorify God in everything we do. This is why we exist—to reflect His glory and bring Him praise.

We don't need to run after the things of the world because we have been given everything we need in Christ. When we understand this, we stop striving for worldly success, and we start living for the eternal. The things of this world are temporary; our life in Christ is eternal.

We are God's creation, born through His truth, and destined to be His firstfruits. Our lives are meant to honor

Him and reflect His glory. We do not need to chase after the empty things of this world, for we have already overcome it through Christ. Our victory is secure, and our purpose is clear: to live for the glory of God. We are called to live in peace, trusting in His provision, and reigning in His victory. As we walk in His truth, we fulfill the purpose for which we were created.

The Living Power of God's Word

"For the word of God is alive and active. Sharper than any double-edged sword, it penetrates even to dividing soul and spirit, joints and marrow; it judges the thoughts and attitudes of the heart."

— Hebrews 4:12

God's word is not just written text; it is alive and powerful. It is sharper than any double-edged sword, capable of cutting through the deepest layers of our lives—our soul, our spirit, and even our hidden thoughts. When we read and reflect on it, God's word does not just stay on the surface; it works deeply within us, revealing the truth about our hearts and guiding our actions.

In practical terms, this means that God's word has the power to transform us. When we face challenges, confusion, or temptation, God's word cuts through the confusion, offering clarity, wisdom, and direction. It exposes our innermost thoughts and motives, showing us where we need to grow and change. It judges not just our actions, but our attitudes.

For example, when we struggle with fear or anxiety, God's promises can pierce our hearts and remind us of His faithfulness. When we face difficult decisions, His word offers wisdom to make choices that honor Him. And in moments of doubt, His word reassures us of His love and purpose for our lives.

The Power of Faith

"Now faith is confidence in what we hope for and assurance about what we do not see."

— **Hebrews 11:1**

Faith is the foundation of our relationship with God. It's not just a feeling; it is a firm belief in things hoped for and the certainty of things unseen. Faith is the bridge between our present reality and God's promises. It is the confidence that what we hope for will come to pass, even if we cannot see it with our physical eyes.

In practical terms, faith means acting as if what we are believing for has already happened. It is not waiting to see the outcome, but stepping out in belief that what we desire is already ours through God's provision. When we believe with unwavering certainty that God will fulfill His promises, we start living as though it has already been accomplished. For instance, if you are praying for healing or a breakthrough in your life, faith means you speak as though you are already healed or already have your answer. It's not about waiting for a physical sign to prove it, but trusting that what you've asked for in prayer is already given by God. If you're seeking peace in a challenging situation, faith means you act in peace, even before the solution is visible. It means resting in the assurance that God is working on your behalf, even if you can't see the outcome yet. Your faith in God's promises gives you the courage to move forward with confidence, knowing He will provide exactly what you need.

When there seems to be no Way

"What is impossible with man is possible with God."
— **Luke 18:27**

There are moments in life when we face situations that seem impossible. Our minds may struggle to find a solution, and our hearts may feel hopeless. We look around, and it feels as though there is no way out—no hope, no way forward. But that is exactly where God's power steps in.

When all human options have been exhausted, and when every possible avenue has been blocked, remember that with God, there is always a way. What seems impossible for us is entirely possible for Him. God is not bound by the limitations we face. His ability to work in our lives is beyond anything we can imagine.

Practical Example:

Think of a moment when you faced a challenge that seemed insurmountable—maybe a relationship problem, financial difficulty, or personal struggle. You may have thought there was no way out. But when you trusted God and surrendered the situation to Him, He made a way. Even when everything seemed hopeless, God opened doors you didn't see coming.

This is the reality of living with faith in God. When we reach the end of our ability, God's power is just beginning. He can provide a way where there seems to be no way, turning what appeared as an impossible situation into a testimony of His greatness.

When you find yourself in a place of hopelessness, remember this truth: What man cannot do, God can. Trust in His ability to make a way when there seems to be none. There is always hope in Him, even when all other hope seems lost. Keep believing, because God specializes in turning the impossible into possible.

Trusting in the Lord – A Life with Jesus
In our lives, we often face moments of doubt, fear, and uncertainty. But in those moments, we are called to place our trust in God, knowing that He is always with us. This chapter is about understanding the power of trusting in Jesus and how He never lets His children down.
The Bible teaches us in Psalm 25:2, *"O my God, I trust in You; let me not be ashamed; let not my enemies triumph over me."* The verse reminds us that when we place our trust in God, He will never allow us to be ashamed or defeated. His love and faithfulness protect us and keep our dignity intact.
Imagine a life where every step you take is guided by trust in the Lord. No matter how difficult the circumstances, you know deep in your heart that Jesus will never let you down. His presence will sustain you, strengthen you, and uphold you in every situation.
When we trust in God, He covers us with His grace and mercy. He does not let us face shame or failure. He lifts us up, even when the world might try to put us down. No matter how challenging life may be, Jesus always ensures

that our honor is preserved. We are never alone when we walk in faith.

There will be times when people may try to undermine us or our abilities. But as we place our trust in Jesus, He becomes our defender. His protection surrounds us like a shield. No matter what others may say or do, He ensures that our reputation remains intact.

In the presence of God, we are never abandoned. We are always under His watchful care. As we trust Him more each day, we learn that we don't have to fight our battles alone. Jesus, our Savior, fights for us and makes sure that we stand tall, with our heads held high.

We must remember: *"He will not let us be ashamed."* When we trust in Jesus, He honors that trust and protects our integrity. So, let us walk with courage, knowing that we have a faithful God who never fails.

As we continue to place our faith in Him, let's declare with confidence, "God is my refuge, my strength, and my protector. I will not be ashamed."

Trusting in His Capabilities – Believing in Divine Strength

In life, we often encounter moments filled with uncertainty, doubt, and fear. But when we place our trust in the Divine, there is no situation too daunting and no challenge too great. Just like an athlete who practices tirelessly, without being concerned about the records or achievements of others, we too must develop a mindset of unwavering belief.

When an athlete trains, they don't focus on the world records or past accomplishments of their competitors.

They don't fear the competition. Instead, they practice with the mindset of *winning*. The key is not fear, but belief in oneself and the process. A player's focus is not on the strength of their opponent but on improving their own skills. They know that by dedicating themselves to practice, their abilities will grow. They believe in themselves, not in the potential for defeat.

Similarly, in life, we should never fear any situation. Challenges are temporary—they will pass. What remains, what is permanent, is the Divine. And once we have recognized and understood this, we must place our full trust in God's abilities. **Trust in the Divine's power**—for when we do this, we realize that nothing is impossible.

Just like an athlete who practices without fear, we must move through life with the same mindset. No situation should make us tremble. Life may present us with difficulties, but we can face them with strength because we trust in the One who is the ultimate source of strength—**God**, through **Jesus**. He empowers us, and with that divine support, we can achieve anything. When we trust in His abilities, we unlock our own potential.

It is essential that we do not doubt, and we do not shy away from challenges. Life may feel overwhelming, but we must stand firm in the knowledge that we are supported by a power far greater than ourselves. **Do not doubt**, for God's power is enough to carry us through any trial.

So, remember this: trust in the Divine's power, and you will find yourself able to do things you once thought impossible. **Through God, through Jesus, all things are**

possible—through Him, we can achieve anything. Keep your faith strong, remain unshaken, and the Divine will guide you through every trial.

Know the Truth, and the Truth Will Set You Free

When we come to know the truth, we are set free. The truth is that **Jesus** is the way, the truth, and the life. Through Him, we have been liberated from every bond, every chain that once held us captive. All our obstacles break down, and every path opens up before us. We are freed from all curses, and every form of limitation disappears. Once we know the truth, we are truly free.

Yet, even today, some believers live in fear despite knowing the truth. They remain trapped in rituals, superstitions, and the misconceptions of good and bad omens. They are entangled in their own delusions and the endless cycle of overthinking. But the truth is, **Jesus** has set us free. Once we embrace the truth, we are liberated from the chains of unnecessary fear and worry.

There are still some who live in mental bondage. Despite knowing the truth, they don't free themselves. We, however, have found freedom the moment we embraced the truth. The truth has transformed our lives. Some continue to live in captivity, but God's word is alive—it is the living word of the Lord, and it is with us.

We are free from all kinds of negative thoughts, pain, sickness, financial struggles, poverty, unemployment, and even the corruption of bad habits. His light has lifted us from the darkness and given us a new life. We are the light of the world, and light reigns over all.

Through **Jesus**, we have been set free, and we stand in His light, liberated from the shadows.

No One Shall Be Barren in Your Land

The Bible clearly promises that "in your land, no one will be barren, and no one will suffer miscarriage" (Exodus 23:26). I have witnessed this truth in my own life and observed how many believers, despite knowing the promises of God, still live in fear. Fear arises when they face challenges in conceiving, or when complications arise during pregnancy. Some even fear if they haven't conceived quickly enough or worry about any health issues during pregnancy.

But the Word of God is clear and offers certainty: *"Whoever trusts in Him will not be moved."* God's promises are not empty; they are filled with assurance. The Lord has given us His word, and that word guarantees that we are never alone, even in our most uncertain times. There is no reason to fear.

Fear should never take root in our hearts. God has assured us that those who place their trust in Him will never be shaken. His word stands as a firm foundation, and when we trust in His promises, we can walk confidently without fear. God has given us His surety through His words, and with that, we know we are protected and blessed in every season of our lives.

So, when fear tries to creep in, remember the promises of God. Trust in His faithfulness, for He is always with us, and His word will never fail.

A Believer's Joyful Spirit

A believer's face should never reflect sadness or despair. A true believer can never appear defeated or downhearted. We, as followers of Christ, are meant to be joyful at all times. **God** has always guided me to never fear or dwell in discouragement. We are meant to live with joy, regardless of the circumstances.

We have power within us because the Holy Spirit has been given to us by the Father. We have already overcome the world through Christ. As believers, we are the body of Christ, and a believer should never carry a face of hopelessness. We have been chosen by God to reflect His glory.

If we are excited and filled with joy, only then can we inspire others. Our enthusiasm and positivity will help uplift those around us. When we embrace the joy that God has given us, we become beacons of His love and strength. So, choose to live in joy, for when we are filled with God's spirit, we carry the light that others need.

Trusting God's Guidance- Experience

Life is filled with practical decisions and moments where we are faced with choices, big and small. In every aspect of life, when we place God at the forefront of our thoughts and actions, He never lets us down. I had an experience recently that really opened my eyes to how important it is to involve God in even the smallest decisions.

I had planned to sell my laptop. I had already made up my mind and even told a few people about it. But as I sat down to pray, something changed. In the quiet of that moment, I felt a gentle prompt in my heart, a reminder from God. It was as if He was saying, "Did you discuss this with me?"

At that moment, I realized how often I make decisions without consulting God first. I had been so sure of my plan that I hadn't even stopped to ask for His guidance. I felt a deep sense of regret. Even though this seemed like a small decision, it was a powerful reminder: we cannot take even a single step in life without God's direction.

We often forget that God, our Heavenly Father, is always there to guide us. He is our Shepherd, and in His name, all our work is done. We need to ask for His help, His wisdom, in every decision we make. Whether it is a major life choice or something as simple as selling a laptop, involving Him in our decisions ensures that we are walking on the right path. This experience reminded me that we don't have to face any challenge alone. When we consult with God, He will lead us to the right answers. With Him by our side, everything will work out for the best.

Understanding God's Heart

In my childhood, I came from a different religious background. My family was very disciplined, religious, and straightforward. I always had one question that bothered me: Why do we pray if things don't always happen the way we ask? When I asked this, the answer I received was always the same — "Our job is to pray, whether God grants it or not, it's His will."

This always seemed very strange to me. I couldn't understand why we were supposed to pray for something if, in the end, it was all in God's hands. As I grew into my teenage years and adulthood, I kept feeling that there was no point in asking for anything at all. Most people would say, "Our job is to ask; the rest is up to Him." But I still thought, if God is the one who gives, why not give when we ask?

Today, I've come to realize the truth about God's nature. I understood that Jesus is the true path, and if we call God our Father, then what kind of Father wouldn't want to fulfill His child's desires? Just like a child feels hungry and asks for food, imagine someone telling the child, "It's up to the Father whether He gives or not." It sounds illogical, right? No father would want to see his child suffer or be in need. Every father desires to see his child happy and fulfilled. Similarly, our Heavenly Father desires to give us what we need. He is not distant or indifferent to our pain and desires. He loves us deeply and wants to provide for us in the best way possible. Understanding this has completely changed the way I approach prayer and God's will in my life.

The Power of Healing

I learned the true meaning of healing from God. Healing, is not just about physical recovery; it represents a complete transformation. When God heals us, it means that every aspect of our lives is made whole. Our homes are healed, our finances are restored, our businesses thrive, our spiritual lives grow, and our health is renewed. Everything becomes *GOOD*—made whole and perfect in His grace.

When Jesus performed healing, it wasn't just about fixing physical ailments. It was about changing the very heart of a person. The transformation of the heart is where true healing begins. Only God can do this deep work in us.

Healing happens by God's power, and it happens in an instant when we call on the name of Jesus Christ. This is something that I've experienced firsthand—when we pray in Jesus' name, healing takes place right then and there.

Jesus promised us that we would do even greater works than He did. He said, "You will do greater things than I have done." And today, through His power, we are able to experience that same ability to heal—whether it's physical, emotional, or spiritual healing. It's not by our strength, but by His power that we are able to bring about transformation in our lives and in others' lives.

A Lesson in True Blessing

I was at a Sunday prayer meeting, and as usual, people were sharing their testimonies. One person stood up to share something that left me reflecting deeply. Their testimony was about a baby girl being born into their family, and how, initially, there was disappointment and even a sense of despair. But despite the challenges, they came to realize that the baby girl was, in fact, a blessing from God.

What struck me as strange was how much of the testimony was focused on the gender of the child. There was this feeling of inequality, as if a baby girl somehow couldn't be as much of a blessing as a boy. This made me wonder—why is there so much division and prejudice around gender? Why do we still see so much discrimination based on whether a child is a boy or a girl?

God has created us in His image, and He made no distinction between male and female. In fact, when God created woman, He took a part of man's own body to make her. If He had wanted to make her lesser or different, He would not have done that. God didn't make any distinction between the genders when He created us.

In His word, God tells us to love our wives as we love ourselves, showing that both men and women are of equal value in His eyes. There should be no discrimination based on gender, especially when it comes to the family or the blessings we receive. A daughter is just as much a blessing as a son, and if we truly believe in God's word, we should never see one as less than the other.

Another thing that struck me as strange is the way people talk about pregnancy. Often, a woman is expected to care for herself and the child during pregnancy, as the child is seen as a blessing from God. But at the same time, there's so much division around the gender of the child, as if one child is more valuable than the other. As believers, we should not let gender define our worth or blessings. We need to be careful in how we think and act, showing wisdom and understanding.

We should never see a daughter or a son as anything less than a precious gift from God. Gender should never determine the value or blessing of a child. As followers of Christ, we must embrace God's creation and see His handiwork in every life, whether male or female.

Trusting God with Our Worries

God always wants to see us happy and at peace. He has taken all our burdens upon Himself, and we are called to rest in His care. As it says in the Bible, "Come to me, all you who are weary and burdened, and I will give you rest" (Matthew 11:28). God wants to take away our worries and give us His peace.

It's truly foolish for anyone to pray and then continue to worry. After we bring our concerns to God in prayer, we must trust that He is in control. Worrying after we've prayed shows a lack of trust in God's ability to take care of us. Once we've prayed, we should leave everything in His hands, knowing that He is our provider and protector.

If we look at nature, we can see how perfectly God cares for everything. Look at the flowers—so beautiful, blooming every day without worry. They don't store up food or hoard resources. Each day, they are refreshed with what they need. Similarly, the birds don't worry about the future. They don't store food for tomorrow; they trust that God will provide for them daily. Have you ever seen a bird storing food in its nest? No, they live freely and trust in God's provision.

Yet, here we are, humans—created in God's image—worrying about everything. We try to store up, plan, and control, but we are still consumed by anxiety. God created us in His likeness, and He has made us so much greater than the birds and flowers. If He cares for them, how much more will He care for us?

After praying, we must let go of our fears and trust that God is taking care of us. We are His creation, and He promises to provide for all our needs. We don't need to carry the weight of worry when we have a loving Father who wants us to rest in His peace.

Learning to Fly

The eagle, one of the most majestic creatures, builds its nest at the highest points, far from any danger. When its chicks are born, the mother eagle does something remarkable. After a certain time, she pushes them out of the nest—not to harm them, but to teach them to fly. At first, the young eagles struggle, but their mother doesn't leave them to fall. If they can't fly on their own, she swoops down, spreads her wings, and lifts them back up, again and again, until they learn to soar on their own.

This process can seem harsh, but it is a way of teaching the eagles to become strong, independent, and capable of flying high. They must trust that they can fly, even when they feel unsure or afraid.

In our own lives, we may find ourselves in situations that feel difficult or uncertain, just like those baby eagles. At times, it may seem like we're being pushed out of our comfort zone, but we must trust that God is always with us. Even when we feel like we're falling, He holds us in His hands. God doesn't leave us to struggle alone; He lifts us up, just like the mother eagle. He allows us to face challenges so we can grow stronger, learn, and soar to new heights.

So, in moments of doubt or difficulty, don't question why it's happening. Trust that God is with you, guiding you and ensuring that you won't fall. Like the eagle's chicks, you too will learn to fly, and with God's help, you will rise above any challenge.

Tithing – The Seed of Blessing

Tithing is much more than a financial obligation; it is a seed that we sow into God's kingdom. Just like a seed planted in the ground, tithing carries the potential for a great harvest, not only in the material sense but in spiritual growth, peace, and God's abundant blessings.

Tithing is not merely about money; it's about offering a portion of what we've received in a spirit of gratitude and worship. When we sow this seed of our earnings, we are planting it into the ground of faith. This act, done with the right heart, carries power to produce a great harvest in our lives. It might not always be a financial return, but it could be peace, joy, opportunities, or spiritual growth. God promises that when we give, He will bless us in ways that go beyond our expectations.

In the Bible, God assures us that He will not let any seed of faith go to waste. "Give, and it will be given to you," Jesus says in Luke 6:38. The seed of tithing is never in vain; it always has the potential to bring forth fruit. God multiplies what we sow—whether it's our finances, our time, or our efforts in His service.

Tithing is an act of trust, a recognition that God is the true provider. It is a declaration that we are stewards of His blessings, not owners. And when we sow this seed, we open the door for God's blessings to flow back into our lives, often in ways we least expect.

So, just as we plant a seed in the ground with the expectation of a harvest, let us also sow our tithes with the same faith and expectancy. For in due time, God will bring forth a harvest that far exceeds what we initially gave. Tithing is not just about the tenth we give, but about the abundance of blessings that God will pour back into our lives.

God's Promises – True and Unfailing

God promises to meet all our needs, to bless us with health, wealth, and peace. He assures us that He will never leave us in sorrow; He will wipe away every tear. His promises are not empty words—they are real and true. Unlike humans, who may fail or turn back on their word, God is unwavering in His commitment to us.

When God speaks, His promises are certain. If He says He will provide, He will provide. If He promises healing, you will be restored. If He assures you of prosperity, He will make a way for you to prosper. God's word is not like that of man, who may change his mind or forget. His promises are sure, and they stand forever.

God does not promise a life without struggles, but He guarantees that He will be with you through it all, ensuring that your needs are met and your burdens are lightened. He is faithful to His word, and because of His faithfulness, you will never be left to cry in despair.

Trust in God's promises, for they are true. He is not a man who would lie or turn away. His word is a rock—unchanging, unfailing, and full of hope. Rest in the assurance that God will fulfill every promise He has made to you, and your heart will never be empty again.

God's Constant Presence in My Life

In my own life, I have always found God by my side. He is with me at every moment, His ear always attentive to my voice, listening with love and care. Just as a mother watches over her child every second, God's gaze is constantly upon us, guiding and protecting us with His love. He is always near, closer than anyone else.

When a child is sick, he seeks comfort from his mother. No toy or game can bring him joy; all he desires is to be held in her arms, to find rest and peace in her embrace. Similarly, in our times of trouble, it is only God who can provide the true comfort and rest that our hearts long for. In times of distress, He holds us close, offering care and peace that the world cannot give.

But often, I have noticed that when people are suffering, they tend to turn to others, sharing their pain with the world, unaware that no human can truly take away their suffering. Only God has the power to heal the wounds of the heart and soul. No matter how much we try to seek solace from others, it is ultimately God's presence and His care that provide true relief.

Whenever you face trouble or pain, go to God. Do not turn to the world, for the world cannot offer what only God can. It is in His arms that we find peace and comfort, not in the fleeting promises of the world.

The Divine Plan for Us

God has designed a beautiful life for us, far beyond what we could imagine. The thoughts that never crossed your mind, the feelings that never touched your heart, are the very things that God has planned for you. His plans for us are full of goodness, love, and peace. It's important to place our complete trust in Him because He knows what is best for us, even when we can't see it ourselves.

When we accepted Jesus Christ as our teacher and Savior and confessed our faith, something profound happened. He freed us from the chains of sin and sorrow. Through Him, we are made whole, and our lives are no longer burdened by past mistakes and pains.

Every experience we go through, every challenge we face, is part of God's perfect plan. He orchestrates everything for our good. The troubles, the tests, and the triumphs we encounter—when we look back, we will realize they were all for our benefit. As we move forward in life, we can rest assured that all that we will experience, in His will, will be good.

God has a way of turning everything, even the painful moments, into something beautiful. By following Him and trusting in His divine plan, we can walk with peace in our hearts, knowing that He is guiding us. His love and grace are always with us, shaping us for something greater than we can understand.

Through Him, we find true freedom, joy, and purpose. And as we trust in His plan, we discover that the best is yet to come.

The Gift of the Beloved Son

Look, God has given us His beloved Son, Jesus Christ, as a sacrifice for us. He was willing to give His life for our salvation, showing us the greatest love ever known. Jesus, the Son of God, came into the world as a human being, not for Himself, but for us.

Despite being rich beyond measure, He became poor for our sake, so that we could be made rich—rich in spirit, in grace, and in eternal life. He took on the poverty of humanity so that we could receive the abundance of God's blessings, becoming spiritually wealthy, beyond what money can offer.

Anyone who places their trust in the Lord, in the Savior, will never consider themselves poor. Even in moments of struggle, a person who believes in God's provision is richer than the wealthiest person in the world. The true richness is in knowing the truth, in accepting Jesus Christ as the Lord and Savior. To accept Him is to recognize the true source of wealth—eternal life, peace, and purpose in the Lord.

Therefore, let us remember, the greatest wealth is not in earthly riches, but in the truth of Jesus Christ. And with Him, we are made truly rich, for He brings us closer to the heart of God.

Life in Christ

In the journey of faith, one of the greatest blessings we have is the guidance of the Holy Spirit. GOD Himself provides us with wisdom and teaches us how to live in Christ. He helps us navigate the challenges of life, showing us how to behave wisely, how to respond in various situations, and how to speak with love and grace.

There are times when we find ourselves in situations where we are unsure of what to say. Our emotions might get the better of us, and we might feel frustrated, angry, or even overjoyed. In those moments, it's easy to say something that we later regret. But we must remember that God is always with us. His Spirit speaks through us and helps us respond with wisdom. He leads us in paths of righteousness and teaches us how to use our words wisely.

One important lesson that God has taught me is this: Never make decisions in excitement, and never speak out of frustration. When you're in a state of extreme joy or deep frustration, it's best to hold your tongue. Often, we say things in the heat of the moment, only to realize later that we shouldn't have spoken at all. Words, once spoken, cannot be taken back. This is why we must always be careful and vigilant about the words we speak.

The Bible reminds us that our words have power – they can build up or tear down. That's why we must strive to speak words that uplift, encourage, and bring glory to God. Whether in moments of joy or sorrow, we should always use our speech to bless others and reflect the love of Christ. Even when things look difficult or negative, we should refrain from speaking harshly or negatively. Instead, we must choose to speak life and hope, trusting that God's Spirit will guide our words.

It's easy to get caught up in our emotions and say things we don't mean, but when we allow the Holy Spirit to lead us, He helps us control our tongue. He teaches us to speak with patience and grace, remembering that our words reflect the heart of Christ. It's a reminder that, as believers, we are called to be salt and light in the world, and that includes how we speak to others.

So, next time you find yourself in a challenging situation, remember that God is with you. Trust in His wisdom, and let His Spirit guide you in everything you say and do. By doing so, you will not only honor God but also bring peace and blessing to those around you. Be mindful of your words, for they hold the power to shape your life and the lives of those you interact with.

May we always speak wisely, with love, and for God's glory

God's Promises Are Always True- Practical

God's promises are steadfast and true. He never lets us be ashamed or humiliated, and He never allows us to bow down to anyone. Before we even ask or think about our needs, He already knows exactly what we require. All we need to do is remain firm in our faith and trust in His timing and provision. His promises are sure, and if we stand in belief, He will fulfill them.

We are called to manifest His promises in our lives. But how do we do this? The Holy Spirit teaches us how to bring those promises to light. He guides us on how to align our lives with God's plan, and how to live in such a way that His promises become visible to others. It's important to stay rooted in Him because when we do, He takes care of everything.

For example, if someone is seeking work or a job, they need to understand that their practical approach matters just as much as their faith. Some people approach the job search as if they're doing others a favor, with a dead or lifeless attitude. But practical work, without faith, is dead. It needs to be alive, driven by belief and purpose. When you believe and walk in faith, your actions speak volumes.

Let me illustrate: if you are looking for a job, adapt a lifestyle that reflects the job you want. Be punctual. If you want a job, start waking up early, preparing your clothes, and getting ready as if you already have the job. Pack your lunch and prepare for the day with excitement and purpose. Do this with a strong belief that you are walking into your destiny, and it will surely become a testimony of God's faithfulness.

God is our Father, and just as any father knows what his children need, God knows what we require even before we ask. A good father would never want his child to struggle or go without. But if we remain passive and go through the motions with a defeated attitude—waking up late, dragging ourselves through the day, and carrying a gloomy face—then nothing will work. Our faith must be active. We need to live out the life we believe in. When we align our actions with our faith, the results will follow.

Take the example of someone wanting to buy a new house. If that is your goal, start living practically as if you already have that home. Begin preparing to move. Pack your things as if you are already shifting to your new place. Speak with authority and faith, declaring that you are moving into your new home. Keep your focus on the goal and refuse to let negative or doubtful thoughts distract you. Trust in God's provision and live as if it is already done.

Practical faith means living as if you are already in possession of what you've asked for. This is the kind of faith that moves mountains. It's not about simply hoping or wishing for things to happen. It's about walking with the belief that God has already provided for you, and you're living in anticipation of what is to come.

But there are times when people waver in their faith. They start off strong, believing in God's promises, but then doubt creeps in. They might say, "I trusted in God, I did what I was supposed to, but it didn't work." But when we examine their actions, we might find that they didn't approach things with honesty or integrity. Faith isn't just about wishing for things to happen; it's about putting in the effort, being diligent, and walking in line with God's will.

Remember the example of Moses. God promised him and the Israelites a land flowing with milk and honey, but they didn't enter that land right away. Why? Because they began to complain and speak negatively. They grew discouraged, murmured, and allowed their faith to weaken. Instead of trusting in God's promise, they doubted and focused on their circumstances. Complaining and grumbling never bring blessings or breakthroughs.

There is no blessing in complaining. There is no success in having a negative attitude. When we learn to be thankful, to focus on God's goodness, and to trust that He is working on our behalf, we will see His promises come to pass in our lives. Even when things don't look like they're going the way we expect, if we remain thankful and continue to walk in faith, God will make a way where there seems to be no way.

So, do not let your faith weaken. Never let your words or actions reflect doubt or frustration. Stay strong, trust in God's promises, and continue to move forward with practical faith. God will not fail you, and He will fulfill every promise He has made to you. Always give thanks, and know that your efforts, coupled with your faith, will bring success. God's promises are always true, and He will never let you down.

My Own Practical Experience in My Life

In my life, I have experienced the power of God's promises in a very real and practical way. I want to share a time when my husband and I were living in a house, and everything seemed uncertain. We were staying at my in-laws' place, and one day, they told us, "You need to leave. This is our house, and you cannot stay here anymore. Empty the room."

At that moment, my husband and I put our trust in God. We knew that our Provider would not abandon us. We packed up everything we owned, leaving only two pieces of clothing out. We didn't have much, but we took action. We knew it was time to go, and we began living with the practical faith that God had a plan for us. We were leaving behind most of our stuff, but we kept our trust in God alive. Our family wanted us to follow their traditions, their customs, and even their idol worship, but we couldn't do that. We didn't believe in it, and because of this, they stopped speaking to us. It was a tough situation, but we continued to hold onto our faith in God. Every day, we repeated, "God is our provider. He will take care of us. We trust in Him."

Even though we didn't have much, we kept declaring that we would have our own home one day. We said, "God has given us a home. We already have our own place, and God will provide." And you know what? He did. One day, God led us to our own home. He took care of everything for us. We didn't know how it would happen, but God made a way.

He gave us our own house, and we truly saw His faithfulness in action.

The Bible says, *"I am the Lord your God, who brought you up out of Egypt; I will open my mouth wide, and I will fill it"* *(Psalm 81:10).* God promises that He will never leave us lacking. When we trust Him and follow His direction, He fills our lives with His blessings. There is no shortage with God. At the time, we had nothing We came to that situation with empty hands, but God brought us through. Today, we have everything more than we need. God has blessed us abundantly, and looking back, I can see how His hand was upon us every step of the way.

It's important to understand that faith in God isn't just about believing in the unseen; it's also about taking practical steps in alignment with that faith. When we act in trust and confidence, God opens doors that we couldn't have imagined. He provides for us in ways we never thought possible.

What I learned through this experience is that God always has a plan for us. Even when the circumstances look bleak, when we are told there is no place for us, when we are misunderstood or rejected, God is still working behind the scenes. If we trust Him, He will make a way where there seems to be no way. And just like He provided a home for us, He will provide for you in every area of your life.

Remember, all we need to do is keep our trust in God, take the practical steps of faith, and watch Him fulfill His promises.

143

Prophecies and the Power of the Mind

Prophecies are not the result of mere human words; they come from the will of God. Sometimes, people might speak over our lives and declare things they believe about our future, but we must always remember that it is God's will that determines what will happen in our lives, not the words of men. When someone prophesies over you, don't take it lightly. Instead, **claim it** and **begin to act upon it practically**. The moment you begin to live according to that prophecy with faith, you align yourself with God's purpose for your life.

For example, if someone prophesies something good for your future, don't just sit back and wait for it to happen. **Start living** as if it's already been fulfilled. Take practical steps that align with that prophecy. When you live with the belief that you have already received, it opens the door for God to move in your life.

"Believe and you will receive." This is a powerful principle. The mind has incredible power over the body. The way we think and believe directly influences our actions and our reality. If your mind is strong, confident, and aligned with God's promises, your body will follow suit. If you wake up in the morning feeling weak, tired, and defeated, and someone tells you that you look sick or weak, your mind will take that thought in, and your body will begin to react according to that belief. But, if your mind refuses to accept defeat, and instead, you command your body to be strong, saying, "I am strong; I am healthy; nothing can harm me," your body will follow your commands.

The mind is the command center of the body. It directs how we feel, how we act, and how we perceive ourselves and our circumstances. When you train your mind to believe in God's promises and to stay strong, no matter what is happening around you, the body will respond accordingly. Even if you are feeling weak or sick, don't let your mind accept defeat. Instead, remind yourself that you are strong in Christ, and He has already given you the victory. Your body will align with your thoughts.

When you are faced with challenges, do not allow your mind to dwell on negativity or defeat. Your mind must remain focused on the promises of God. **If your mind is focused on God's goodness and strength, your life will reflect that.** The mind cannot be passive. It must be actively engaged in declaring God's truths over your life.

If you're feeling sad or discouraged, don't give in to those feelings. Instead, choose to focus on the joy of the Lord and the hope He has placed in you. When your mind is focused on the promises of God, it will not allow sadness or fear to take hold. **Choose to be happy in the Lord**, knowing that He is in control, and trust that He will guide you through every situation.

Your thoughts are powerful. What you choose to believe, what you choose to speak, and how you choose to think will dictate your reality. When you keep your mind strong, positive, and rooted in God's truth, your life will reflect His peace, joy, and victory.

So, whenever a prophecy is spoken over your life, don't just listen and wait for it to unfold. **Live it out.** Act on it. Command your mind to align with what God has said about you, and begin to walk in the confidence that you already have what God has promised. Your faith will unlock the power of God to bring those prophecies to pass.

Remember, **the mind gives commands to the body**. If your mind is weak and full of doubt, your body will reflect that. But if your mind is strong in faith and aligned with God's truth, your body will also respond with strength and vitality. Always command your mind to focus on the goodness of God, and your body will follow.

Blessings for Obedience

There are times when we question ourselves about how to live in obedience to God. What does it really mean to be obedient to God? What should our behavior look like in His presence, and how do we reflect that in our daily lives? God has taught me a lot about this, and I want to share one experience that opened my eyes to the importance of obedience and how our actions should align with His will.

I remember once attending a fellowship at a resort. The experience that unfolded there left me with a lesson that still resonates deeply in my heart. As believers, we often have a strong sense of community within the church. We're encouraged to be kind, loving, and supportive to one another. But sometimes, we forget to reflect those same values when we step outside of the church environment. I had asked myself, "How do we behave when we're not in fellowship with other believers? How do we represent Christ when we're in the world?"

During our time at the resort, I had to use the restroom. When I walked in, I was shocked by how dirty and unkempt it was. The housekeeping lady was there, and she seemed very frustrated. She said to me, "Madam, look at the condition here. These people, when they leave, they don't even care to clean up after themselves. They just go around doing whatever they want. And when we say something, they respond by saying, 'You don't get paid enough for this.'"

That moment hit me hard. Here we were, as believers, in a fellowship setting, supposedly representing Christ, and yet we were not behaving in a way that reflected His love and purity. I couldn't help but think, "What do people outside the church think of us? When they see us in action, how do they perceive our behavior?" The behavior of some individuals in that place was far from the love and kindness that God calls us to exhibit. I realized that our actions, especially in public, matter just as much as what we do in the church. We are the light of the world, and our conduct in every situation should reflect Christ.

In that moment, I was reminded of something very important: **our behavior should be a testimony to everyone around us.** The Bible says, *"Your gentleness should be evident to all" (Philippians 4:5).* It doesn't say it should be evident just to fellow believers, but to *all* people. As followers of Christ, we need to show the world that we are different by how we treat others, especially in situations where we might feel frustrated or upset.

When I saw how some of the guests at the resort were treating the service staff—shouting at them, speaking rudely, and not showing any respect for the people serving them—it struck me. This behavior wasn't just disrespectful; it was completely opposite to what Christ teaches us. As believers, we are called to serve others with humility and kindness, not to treat them as if they are beneath us.

The Lord commands us to honor those around us, regardless of their position or role in life. We are called to be lights in a dark world, and our obedience to God is reflected in how we treat others. Whether we're in the church, at work, or in a public place, our behavior should always bring glory to God.

I realized that obedience to God is not just about following the rules or attending church services; it's about living out His commands in every area of our lives. It's about reflecting His love, His humility, and His gentleness in all our interactions. **Obedience to God is a lifestyle, not just a Sunday activity.**

The Bible teaches us that *"Your gentleness will be evident to all"* (Philippians 4:5). That means, if we are truly walking in obedience to God, our lives will reflect His love, kindness, and compassion to everyone, not just those who are believers. People will see Christ in us through the way we act, the way we speak, and the way we treat others.

After that experience, I couldn't help but think about how we, as believers, need to change our mindset and our behavior when we're out in the world. If we are truly living in obedience to God, our conduct should reflect His character. We need to be mindful of how we speak to others, how we treat people in positions of service, and how we represent Christ in every situation.

In the end, it's about letting God's word transform us from the inside out. When we live in obedience, our actions will naturally align with His will, and that will be a testimony to those around us. Let us remember that our behavior, in every setting, should reflect the love of Christ and be a shining example to the world. **Obedience brings blessings,**

and those blessings are evident in how we live and interact with others.

Let us strive to live in a way that honors God and draws others to Him. Our obedience can make a powerful impact on the world around us.

Blessings for Obedience

If you fully obey the LORD your God and carefully follow all his commands I give you today, the LORD your God will set you high above all the nations on earth. **2** All these blessings will come on you and accompany you if you obey the LORD your God:

The Blessings of Obedience

One of the most powerful truths in the Bible is that **obedience to God brings blessings**. In Deuteronomy 28:1, it says, *"If you fully obey the LORD your God and carefully follow all His commands..."* This is a conditional promise—God's blessings are tied to our willingness to obey Him. If we obey His commands and follow His ways, we position ourselves to receive the fullness of His blessings in our lives. But what does it mean to fully obey God? It's not just about following the rules or ticking off a checklist. Obedience is about **being in His presence**, letting His Word dwell in us, and aligning our hearts with His will. When we remain rooted in His Word, when His promises become our reality, we will see His blessings unfold in our lives.

God's Word teaches us that when we obey, we step into His plan for us—a plan that includes His love, peace, and prosperity. But here's the key: **obedience is the**

foundation. Everything else follows when we make the choice to obey Him, live according to His commands, and trust in His goodness.

The Promise of Blessings

God promises that when we obey Him, He will bless us. In Deuteronomy 28:3-6, He speaks of blessings that cover every area of our lives:

- *"You will be blessed in the city and blessed in the country."*
- *"The fruit of your womb will be blessed, and the crops of your land and the young of your livestock—the calves of your herds and the lambs of your flocks."*
- *"Your basket and your kneading trough will be blessed."*
- *"You will be blessed when you come in and blessed when you go out."*

These are not just empty promises—they are declarations of the fullness of God's blessing on our lives. When we are obedient to Him, His blessings are sure to follow. Whether we are in the city or in the country, whether at work or at home, we are blessed because we have aligned ourselves with God's will.

God's blessings are not limited to just spiritual matters. He cares about our **physical needs** as well. He promises to bless our **families**, our **work**, and our **daily provision**. When we walk in obedience, He ensures that we have what we need. Our work will be fruitful, our relationships will be blessed, and we will have more than enough.

A Life of Freedom and Joy

God doesn't want us to live in a constant struggle or to be weighed down by the burdens of this world. He wants us to live freely, joyfully, and abundantly. **"He who the Son sets free is free indeed."** (John 8:36) God has already provided everything we need, and His desire is for us to live in the fullness of His love, not in lack or limitation.

The luxuries of the world are not what should define us. While material things are nice, they are not the source of true joy or fulfillment. True peace and joy come from being rooted in God's love and obeying His commands. When we live in obedience to Him, we find ourselves **living in His perfect freedom**. We are not burdened by fear or doubt, but we live in the freedom that comes from trusting in His provision and promises.

God's Love for Us

God's love for us is unconditional and everlasting. He is always ready to bless us, always ready to provide for us, and always willing to guide us. **We are His beloved children**, and He desires only good for us. His commands are not burdensome but are meant to lead us into a place of peace, abundance, and joy.

As His children, we must prepare our hearts to receive His blessings. God is always ready to give, but we must be ready to receive. That readiness comes through obedience. When we make the decision to align our will with His, we are opening ourselves to His blessings in every area of life.

Walking in Obedience

Living in obedience is a choice. It's a choice to trust God's plan, to believe His Word, and to walk in His ways. When we obey, **we are positioning ourselves for success**. No matter what challenges come our way, God's promises remain sure. He has promised that when we obey, we will be blessed in everything we do. Whether coming in or going out, our lives will be marked by His favor.

Let us commit to living lives of obedience. Let us trust God, follow His commands, and walk in the knowledge that His blessings will follow us. **Obeying God is not just about rules—it's about positioning ourselves to experience His love and blessings in our everyday lives.**

When we fully obey God, we open the door for His divine blessings. It's a life of freedom, joy, and prosperity. And as we continue to walk in obedience, we will experience more of His goodness and faithfulness in every area of our lives. **Obey, and you will be blessed.**

Guarding Your Mind and Heart

There are times when we get so caught up in our own thoughts, lost in the endless cycle of worries and fears, that our minds begin to spiral. We become so overwhelmed by these negative thoughts that they slowly turn into fear, and this fear starts to control our actions and words. In these moments, we may find ourselves saying things we regret or taking actions that don't align with who we truly are. And then, we might blame others or external forces, saying, *"The enemy made me do this,"* or *"This happened because of the evil around me."*

But the reality is different. It's not always the external world that is to blame. It's not always the "devil" or bad influences that cause us to act out of line. More often than not, **we open the door to these negative forces ourselves**. We leave room for doubt, fear, and negativity to creep into our hearts and minds.

I've seen this happen in many lives. People begin to believe that their circumstances are controlling them, but in reality, they are the ones who allowed fear and doubt to take root. We leave our minds open to any thought, any fear, and, in doing so, we invite negativity in. Just like leaving a door unlocked invites an intruder into your home, leaving your mind open to negativity invites fear, doubt, and wrong thinking into your life.

This is why it is so crucial to **guard our hearts and minds**. Proverbs 4:23 says, *"Above all else, guard your heart, for everything you do flows from it."* Our thoughts shape our emotions, and our emotions drive our actions. If we allow fear, doubt, or anger to dominate our minds, we will eventually see those emotions play out in our lives.

So, how do we prevent this from happening? How do we stop ourselves from falling into the trap of fear and negativity?

Guard Your Mind

The first step is to **be aware of what you allow into your mind**. Just like you wouldn't leave your door open for a thief to walk in, you shouldn't leave your mind open to every thought that comes your way. Not every thought that crosses your mind is worth entertaining. We must choose what we allow to stay in our minds.

When negative or fearful thoughts come, we must be quick

to recognize them and **reject them**. If you allow fear, doubt, or negativity to linger, it will begin to take root in your mind. Instead, **replace those thoughts with truth**. The Bible tells us to *"take captive every thought to make it obedient to Christ"* (2 Corinthians 10:5). When you feel fear or anxiety creeping in, replace those thoughts with God's promises. Fill your mind with His Word and with thoughts of hope, peace, and faith.

Be Attentive to Your Thoughts

It's not enough to simply avoid letting bad thoughts into your mind. We must also be **attentive** to what we're thinking about. Are you focusing on problems, worries, or things that haven't even happened yet? Or are you focusing on the goodness of God and His faithfulness? The more we focus on God's promises, the less room we leave for fear and doubt to settle in.

Be watchful over your thoughts and emotions. Stay conscious of what's taking root in your heart. Don't let negativity or fear take hold. Keep your mind sharp, focused, and aligned with God's Word. If you catch yourself thinking negative or fearful thoughts, take immediate action to turn your thoughts around.

Don't Give Access to Fear

Fear is one of the most dangerous things we can allow into our minds. It's the root of so many destructive thoughts and actions. The Bible reminds us that **God has not given us a spirit of fear**, but of power, love, and a sound mind (2 Timothy 1:7). Fear does not come from God—it comes from the enemy, and it only serves to paralyze us, keeping us from walking in faith and victory.

When you allow fear into your heart, you give it control over your actions and words. Fear can cause you to say things you don't mean or act in ways that are harmful to yourself and others. That's why it's so important to **guard against fear**. When fear tries to enter your mind, speak God's promises out loud. Remind yourself that God is in control, and His love casts out all fear (1 John 4:18).

Close the Doors to Negativity

Remember, you are the one who decides what you allow into your mind. If you don't want fear, negativity, or wrong thoughts to take root, then **close the door** to them. Don't give them an opportunity to enter. You can do this by staying vigilant in your thoughts, being quick to reject negative influences, and always turning to God's Word for truth and guidance.

The key to living in peace and victory is to **guard your mind**. When you protect your mind from negativity, fear, and doubt, you are protecting your peace and your future. **Your thoughts shape your life.** If you allow negativity to control your thoughts, it will eventually control your actions. But if you guard your heart and mind, focusing on God's truth and His promises, you will walk in victory.

So, next time you feel overwhelmed or fearful, remember: you have the power to control your thoughts. Don't let the enemy have a foothold in your mind. Don't leave the door open to negativity, fear, or doubt. **Guard your mind**, and your heart will follow. Fill your thoughts with God's truth, His love, and His promises. Stay vigilant, and you will see the power of your thoughts transform your life.

Take control of your mind, and you'll take control of your future.

Calming the Storm of Your Thoughts with Authority

There are times in life when we feel as though everything is spiraling out of control, when storms of fear, anxiety, and confusion rise within us, just as they did on the Sea of Galilee. In the Bible, we see a powerful example of Jesus calming a literal storm, but what if I told you that you have the same authority to calm the storm within your own heart and mind?

In the Gospel of Matthew, we read the story of Peter walking on water. Jesus, in the middle of a storm, was walking on the water toward His disciples. Peter, amazed and full of faith, asked Jesus if he could also walk on the water. Jesus said, *"Come."* Peter stepped out of the boat and began to walk toward Jesus. But as he walked, something happened—he began to sink. Why? The Bible says that Peter's focus shifted. Instead of keeping his eyes on Jesus, he looked around at the storm and the wind, and fear began to overwhelm him.

When Peter took his eyes off Jesus, he began to doubt. His focus shifted from Jesus, the one with all authority, to the storm, and that fear caused him to lose his footing. Just like Peter, when we allow our focus to shift away from God, we begin to sink into the storms of life.

But here's the key—**as long as we keep our focus on Jesus, we can walk through any storm without fear.** Jesus demonstrated His power over the storm by commanding it to be still. He calmed the wind and the waves with a simple word. In that moment, He showed His disciples that **nothing in this world—no storm, no obstacle, no challenge—has authority over God**. And the same power that was in Jesus is available to you and me today.

The Power of Focus

Peter's faith was strong as long as his focus remained on Jesus. When he saw the storm, when he took his eyes off Jesus, fear crept in and his faith wavered. This is a vital lesson for us: **where you focus your attention will determine the direction of your life.**

If you focus on the storm—on the difficulties, the uncertainties, and the fears of life—you will begin to sink. But if you keep your eyes on Jesus, who is the Master of the storm, you will be able to walk through anything with authority and peace.

Think about it: when we focus too much on the news, on what's going wrong in the world, on the problems in our lives, we allow those things to control our thoughts and our emotions. Fear starts to rise, and before we know it, we feel overwhelmed and helpless. The more we allow our minds to dwell on these external storms, the more we invite fear to rule over us.

Command the Storm with Authority

Just as Jesus spoke with authority and calmed the storm, you too have been given authority over the storms of your mind. **You have the power to speak peace into your thoughts and calm the raging storm within.**

When fear, doubt, and worry rise up in your mind, you don't have to accept them. You can speak to your mind and command peace, just as Jesus commanded the wind and waves to be still. Jesus lives in you, and the same authority He has, you have access to.

You have the authority to command your thoughts to align with God's truth. When anxiety rises, speak to it. When fear threatens to overwhelm you, speak peace over your mind. **Speak with the authority of a child of God.**

Your identity in Christ is one of victory, peace, and authority. You are not a victim of your circumstances; you are more than a conqueror through Christ. The storms of life may come, but you have been given the power to stand firm, to be still, and to command peace.

Guarding Your Focus

It is essential to keep your focus on God. When you fix your eyes on Him, you will have peace, no matter what storms are raging around you. This doesn't mean the storms will disappear immediately, but it does mean that you will have the strength and peace to navigate through them.

Remember, **you are not like the world.** While others may be tossed around by fear and uncertainty, you have already been given the victory through Christ. **You are a victorious person who cannot be defeated.** You have authority over your thoughts, over your emotions, and over every storm that comes your way.

You are a child of God, and nothing in this world has the power to defeat you unless you allow it. Don't let fear, doubt, or anxiety rule your life. Instead, **walk with authority**. Calm the storm within, and watch as peace takes over your heart and mind.

When the storms of life come, you have a choice: you can focus on the chaos and sink into fear, or you can focus on Jesus, the one who calms every storm. Keep your eyes on Him, and you will walk through the storm with confidence, authority, and peace.

As a child of God, you have been given authority over your thoughts and circumstances. Just as Jesus calmed the literal storm, you can calm the storm in your mind. Speak with authority, command peace, and trust that God is with you, guiding you through every challenge. **You are more than a conqueror**, and with Jesus by your side, you can never fail. Keep your focus on Him, and the storm will subside.

Life in Christ - Inspiring One Another to Progress

In the journey of life, as followers of Christ, we are called to inspire one another toward progress and growth, not just in terms of achievements but in character, love, and grace. Our actions, words, and attitudes should reflect the life of Christ within us. There was a time when a grievance case involving staff was brought to me for settlement. It was a situation where one staff member had a complaint about another, and it needed resolution.

When I spoke to the concerned person, I asked, "Why do you behave this way? Why don't you speak to your senior in charge directly?" To this, she responded, "I don't like it. My heart refuses to engage in this." I paused for a moment, reflecting on her response, and then I said, "But you claim to be a Christian. And as a Christian, you should know that we are called to love one another. Christians don't act this way. They show love, kindness, and respect to all."

I reminded her, "Remember, God has taught us to love everyone. He showed us the greatest love by sending His beloved Son, Jesus Christ, to die for us. This is the love we are supposed to mirror in our lives. Look at how He loved us even when we were undeserving. What are we doing if we hold personal grudges and let our egos lead us?"

I continued, "Personal grievances, unresolved conflicts, and ego struggles do not belong in the life of a Christian. We are called to live differently. We should respect and love one another, just as Christ does. If we profess to be Christians, we need to ensure our words and actions reflect the love He has shown us. It's not enough to just say we are Christians – we must live as Christ lived."

As I reflected on this moment, I realized that many people say they are Christians, but their actions do not reflect the teachings of Christ. It's easy to claim the title, but much harder to embody the life of Christ. Jesus himself warned that many are called, but few are chosen. To be chosen means to live according to the principles of love, humility, and selflessness that He exemplified.

Being a Christian means allowing Christ to live through us in all aspects of our lives – in how we treat others, how we resolve conflicts, and how we contribute to the growth of those around us. We are meant to be the instruments of God's love, to encourage others, and to help them progress. This progression isn't just about personal success but about fostering a community where everyone can thrive spiritually, emotionally, and socially.

In the end, our mission as Christians is clear: we are called to be a source of encouragement and progress for others, not just through words but through actions. The life of Christ in us should make us agents of change, inspiring one another toward greater love, kindness, and respect. This is how we can make a difference in the world – by living as Christ did and inspiring others to do the same

Don't Be a Stumbling Block for Others

In our daily interactions with others, it is important to remember that our words and actions can have a powerful impact on those around us. As followers of Christ, we are called to be instruments of peace, kindness, and love, not to cause hurt or become a stumbling block in someone else's path.

Sometimes, without even realizing it, we may speak words or take actions that wound others. It could be a sharp comment, a careless joke, or even a harsh criticism. While we may not intend to hurt, the effect can be deep and long-lasting on someone's heart. This is why we must be constantly mindful of how we treat others, because our behavior can either uplift or tear down.

I remember a situation where I witnessed someone saying something to another person that caused them great pain. The words, though perhaps meant casually, struck deep into the heart of the person they were directed at. I immediately saw the sadness in their eyes. It reminded me of how easy it is to hurt someone without thinking, even when we have no ill intentions.

As I reflected on this, I felt a strong conviction. **We are never called to be a stumbling block for others.** In fact, we should be the exact opposite – a source of encouragement, support, and strength for those around us. The Bible teaches us to be mindful of our words, as they hold the power to give life or to bring death. Proverbs 18:21 says, "The tongue has the power of life and death, and those who love it will eat its fruit."

In every conversation and interaction, we must remember that our words can either build up or break down. If we are not careful, we can leave others feeling defeated, hurt, or discouraged. And once a word is spoken, it cannot be taken back, no matter how much we regret it.

Jesus himself was a perfect example of how we should treat others. He never used His words to hurt, belittle, or judge. Instead, He spoke words of love, encouragement, and healing. He reached out to the broken, the marginalized, and those who were suffering. He showed us how to lift others up, not tear them down.

If we claim to be followers of Christ, our actions must reflect His love. We are called to speak life into others, to encourage them in their faith, and to build them up in love.

Let us make it our goal, then, to speak words that heal, comfort, and bring peace, rather than words that hurt or cause division.

There may be times when we disagree with someone, or when we feel frustrated with their actions, but this is no excuse to speak words that harm. Even in our disagreements, we must strive to express ourselves with grace, understanding, and respect. We must be quick to listen, slow to speak, and slow to anger, as James 1:19 reminds us.

We should also be cautious of becoming a stumbling block for others by leading them into temptation or causing them to fall away from their faith. Our actions and behavior should always point others toward Christ, not away from Him. In Romans 14:13, Paul urges us, "Therefore let us stop passing judgment on one another. Instead, make up your mind not to put any stumbling block or obstacle in the way of a brother or sister."

The essence of being a Christian is to love others as Christ has loved us. This means treating others with kindness, respect, and compassion. It means using our words to build others up, rather than tear them down. It means being careful not to cause someone else to stumble in their faith, but to help them grow and thrive.

As we continue our journey of faith, let us always remember the responsibility we have to those around us. Let us choose our words wisely, and let us be careful with our actions. Let us be a source of encouragement, peace, and love for everyone we meet. For in doing so, we reflect the love of Christ to the world around us, and we become a true witness of His grace and mercy.

In conclusion, we must strive to be people who inspire others to live better lives, not people who discourage or hurt. Let us never be a stumbling block, but instead, let us be a stepping stone that helps others rise higher and closer to the heart of God.

Trusting God's Promise in the Face of Trials

The True Nature of Testing

When we go through difficult times, we often hear the phrase, "This is God testing me," or "My trial is from God." But is that really the case? Is every trial, every challenge, truly a test sent by God to test our faith? The truth is, **God does not test us in the way we often think.** He does not bring suffering into our lives as a way to prove something to Himself. Rather, the struggles we face are often a result of our own fears and human limitations.

Take, for example, the case of a woman who is pregnant. If she behaves normally, stays calm, and trusts in the natural process of pregnancy, everything will likely proceed as expected. However, if she begins to worry excessively, constantly fearing what might happen to her baby, that fear can affect her physically and emotionally. **This fear creates stress, which in turn, affects her body.** This nervousness can lead to unnecessary complications, because when we focus on fear rather than faith, we open ourselves to the possibility of the very things we fear.

Now, this is not to say that we should ignore the realities of life or the challenges we face. It is important to acknowledge difficulties and face them with wisdom. But we must also remember that **fear and anxiety often do more harm than the actual challenges themselves.** God's Word encourages us to trust Him and rely on His promises, knowing that He is always with us, guiding us through every storm.

Trusting God's Promises

Let us look at God's promises in His Word. One of the most comforting truths we find in the Bible is that **God is always with us, even in the midst of our trials.** When the Bible says, "No weapon formed against you will prosper," we are reminded that **God's protection and provision are sure.** But how often do we truly live by this promise?

Imagine if a pregnant woman, instead of succumbing to fear, instead chose to meditate on the promises of God. If she were to remember that **God says, "There shall be no miscarriage in your land,"** (Exodus 23:26) she could hold onto the faith that no matter what the circumstances, God is in control. **His Word is true and powerful, and His promises are reliable.**

When we choose to focus on God's promises, we allow His peace to reign in our hearts and minds. The more we align our thoughts with His Word, the less power fear has over us. This does not mean we ignore the challenges, but it does mean we face them with a confidence rooted in the understanding that **God is faithful to His promises.**

Overcoming Fear with Faith

Fear is a powerful force. It can paralyze us and prevent us from stepping into the future that God has planned for us. But the Bible is clear that **fear is not from God.** In 2 Timothy 1:7, we are reminded, "For God has not given us a spirit of fear, but of power, love, and a sound mind." When we experience fear, it is not a sign that God is testing us; it is a signal that we need to turn our focus back to Him, to trust in His Word, and to resist the lies that fear whispers to our hearts.

A critical part of overcoming fear is recognizing that it is often based on lies. We may fear the unknown, or we may fear that things will go wrong, but God has promised to be with us through every trial. **He promises that He will never leave us nor forsake us (Hebrews 13:5).** Fear grows when we begin to doubt God's love and faithfulness, but faith grows when we choose to trust in God's character, even when circumstances seem uncertain.

When we face challenges, we have a choice: we can either let fear dictate our response, or we can choose to stand firm on God's Word, trusting that He is always with us and that His plans for us are good. Fear will only have control over us if we allow it. But when we choose to trust in God's promises, **we step into His peace and experience His strength.**

The Power of Faith Over Fear

Faith is not about ignoring our fears or pretending everything is fine when it is not. Faith is about acknowledging our fears and choosing to trust God with them. When we trust God, we are saying, "Lord, I believe You are bigger than my fears, and I believe You will guide me through this."

Think about a woman who, in her pregnancy, chooses to trust in God's promises rather than give in to fear. When she faces any uncertainty, she remembers that **God has promised to protect her and her baby.** Instead of allowing her fear to take over, she speaks God's promises over her life. She trusts that God is in control, and that no matter what happens, He is with her every step of the way.

This principle is not just true for pregnancy; it applies to every area of life. When we are faced with challenges, **we must choose to trust in God and His Word.** God is not the one sending the testing or suffering. **Our struggles often come from our own fears, doubts, or the challenges we face in this world.** But God has given us the tools to overcome them – His Word, His promises, and His presence.

The Strength to Stand Firm

In the face of trials, we are not meant to stand in our own strength. We are meant to rely on God's strength. The Bible says, "The Lord is my strength and my shield; my heart trusts in Him, and He helps me" (Psalm 28:7). When we feel weak, we can turn to God and find the strength we need to endure.

It is also important to remember that **fear is a choice, but so is faith.** Each day, we are faced with the opportunity to choose which mindset we will adopt. Will we choose to focus on our fears, or will we choose to stand firm in faith, trusting that God is working all things together for our good (Romans 8:28)?

We can be assured that, no matter what we face, **God's Word is our anchor**. His promises are unshakable, and His love for us is constant. When we face difficulties, we can choose to rest in His promises and trust that He is always in control.

Walking in Faith, Not Fear

In the end, the key to overcoming fear is walking in faith. God does not bring suffering or tests into our lives to harm us. **We often suffer because of our own fears, doubts, and uncertainties.** But when we choose to focus on God's promises and trust in His plan, we can find peace in the midst of any storm.

Let us not be controlled by fear, but instead, let us live by faith, trusting that **God is always with us** and that He will guide us through every challenge. We can walk confidently, knowing that **God's promises will never fail.**

As you face your own trials, remember to focus on God's Word, to trust in His promises, and to let His peace guard your heart. Fear will not have the final word in your life – **faith will.**

Love in Action – Our Behavior Reveals Everything

"Little children, let us not love in word or talk but in deed and in truth." – 1 John 3:18

These words from the Bible remind us that love is not merely a sentiment or something we express with words. **True love is demonstrated through our actions.** It's easy to say, "I love you," or to make promises that sound good in the moment, but the real test of love comes when we show it through what we do and how we treat others. Our actions speak louder than our words, and they reveal what is truly in our hearts.

In life, it's not enough to merely talk about love or to claim that we care for someone. If our actions don't match our words, then our love becomes hollow. **It's through our actions that the world sees who we truly are** and how much we are influenced by the love of Christ. When we love in deed and truth, we allow our actions to reflect the depth of our hearts, creating a real and lasting impact on those around us.

I can personally relate to this principle. **My behavior used to be very different.** In the past, I was quick to judge others and slow to forgive. If someone wronged me, I had little patience or tolerance. I would hold grudges, and I often found it difficult to let go of negative feelings. My attitude was driven by ego, frustration, and a desire to be right, and it showed in my actions.

But over time, as I grew in my relationship with Christ, I began to understand that **true love and peace come from within.** It's not about acting out of anger or pride but choosing to act with kindness, patience, and understanding. **This transformation wasn't immediate**—it required a change in mindset, a new way of thinking about how I interacted with others. But little by little, I began to notice a shift. Where I once would have lashed out or become upset, I now found myself staying calm, being more patient, and even showing empathy toward others. I went from being someone who struggled to tolerate others' mistakes to someone who could forgive and move on with peace in my heart.

This process of transformation didn't just come from trying harder. It came from recognizing that **God's love, shown through Christ, is what enables us to truly love others**. As we grow closer to Him, our hearts are softened, and our attitudes begin to change. We start to see the world through the lens of Christ's love rather than through our own selfish desires. As a result, we are able to act in ways that reflect His grace, kindness, and mercy.

For example, when someone wrongs us today, instead of reacting with anger, I try to remember that we are all imperfect, and we all make mistakes. I remind myself that **God has forgiven me for so much**, and therefore, I should forgive others. Instead of holding onto bitterness or frustration, I now choose to offer grace and show love. This is the transformation that happens when we choose to love others in deed and in truth, not just with words.

Our behavior speaks volumes. **It reveals what's truly in our hearts and shows whether or not we are genuinely living out our faith.** When we act out of love, we invite others to experience the love of God through us. People are watching us, whether we realize it or not, and our actions are often the most powerful witness of our faith.

Love in action isn't just about the big moments—it's about the small, everyday interactions with those around us. It's about choosing patience when someone cuts us off in traffic, offering a kind word to someone who's having a tough day, or choosing to listen when someone needs to talk. **Love is in the details** of how we treat others, how we serve them, and how we show them Christ's love through our actions. Our words may fade, but our actions leave a lasting impression.

As I reflect on my own journey, I realize that **my growth in love has been a direct result of learning to act differently**—to choose kindness over frustration, patience over anger, and forgiveness over resentment. It's not always easy, and it's not always quick, but with God's help, it's possible to demonstrate the love He has given us through our actions. **And when we do that, we reflect His glory** in the world around us.

In this chapter, I want to encourage you to reflect on your own actions and behavior. **Are your actions matching your words?** Are you showing love in deed and in truth, or are your actions saying something different? **Our actions reveal who we are** and whether or not we are truly living out the love that God has called us to share with others.

Remember, love is not just a feeling or something we speak; **it's something we do**. And in doing so, we become a living testimony of God's love in the world, showing others what it means to live in His truth and grace. Let's strive to love in action, letting our behavior reflect the heart of Christ and leaving a lasting impact on the lives of those around us.

The Power of Confession and Salvation

"If you declare with your mouth, 'Jesus is Lord,' and believe in your heart that God raised Him from the dead, you will be saved." – Romans 10:9

The day we declare with our mouths, "Jesus is Lord," and believe in our hearts that God raised Him from the dead, **we are saved.** This powerful truth is the foundation of our salvation. It is the moment when we move from death to life, from darkness to light, when we embrace the grace and mercy of God through the sacrifice of His Son, Jesus Christ. Salvation is a gift, given freely to all who confess and believe.

However, declaring Jesus as Lord is only the beginning. **It's not just about saying the words; it's about living them.** Salvation doesn't end with the confession; it's a continuous journey of faith, transformation, and obedience. But the challenge is that even after receiving this incredible gift, **many of us may fall back into sin**, forgetting God's commands, and drifting away from His truth. When we slip into sin, we cannot blame God for our actions. We cannot say that God has failed us or that His gift wasn't enough.

Why? Because **God gave His only Son for us**. He sacrificed His perfect and beloved Son, Jesus, so that we could be saved. He paid the ultimate price, the price of blood, for our redemption. Jesus didn't just die to forgive our past sins, but He died to break the power of sin over us. The moment we declare Him as Lord and believe in our hearts,

God graciously saves us—**this is His free gift to us**. It's a gift that costs us nothing but cost God everything.

God has given us everything we need to live a life of victory over sin. **Jesus paid the price for our freedom**—His life, His blood, His suffering on the cross. And yet, even after receiving this precious gift, some of us choose to turn back to sin. We may forget His commands, ignore His Word, or live as though His sacrifice means nothing. But this is where we must understand that **it is not God who has failed us—it is we who have chosen to walk away.**

When we fall into sin again, it's not because God's grace has run out or because His sacrifice wasn't enough. **It is because we have turned our back on the very One who saved us**. Jesus gave His life to free us from sin, and **we are called to live in that freedom, to honor the sacrifice He made for us by walking in His ways**. His grace is abundant, but it's not meant to be taken lightly. It's not meant to be a license to keep living in sin. When we know the cost of salvation—the blood of Jesus—we should never treat it as something cheap or insignificant.

Jesus didn't just save us for the sake of saying, "You're saved, now go live however you want." He saved us so that **we can live a life that honors Him,** one that reflects the change that has happened within us. **Our salvation is meant to change us**, to transform us into the image of Christ. And even when we stumble, we must remember that **Jesus paid the price for our redemption,** and His mercy is available to us every time we turn back to Him.

It's important to remember that God's love for us is unconditional, but His expectations for our lives are clear. He gave His Son as the ultimate price for our salvation, but He also calls us to live in obedience to Him. **When we stray away from His commands, we cannot blame God for our failures**. Instead, we must recognize that God has already given us all that we need to live a godly life. He has empowered us with His Spirit, provided us with His Word, and set us free from the power of sin.

God's sacrifice for us is not in vain. The cross was not just a historical event; it is the foundation of our daily lives. It's a reminder that, while we were still sinners, Christ died for us. **His sacrifice made salvation possible, but it is up to us to walk in that salvation with integrity, faith, and obedience.**

When we confess Jesus as Lord and believe in our hearts, **we are saved, but the journey doesn't end there.** Salvation is not just about a momentary declaration; it's about an ongoing relationship with Jesus, growing in faith, and living according to His Word. **We must not take God's grace for granted**, but strive each day to live in a way that honors the price He paid for us.

So, let us not forget the incredible gift we have received. Let us not return to the very sins that Jesus died to free us from. Let us live as those who understand the cost of salvation, and live in a way that reflects our gratitude for His sacrifice. God has already given us everything we need, and we are called to honor that gift with our lives.

Remember, salvation is a gift, but living it out requires our active participation. **It requires our obedience, our commitment, and our constant pursuit of God's will for our lives.** When we live in the light of His sacrifice, we show the world that Jesus is truly Lord—not just in word, but in deed and truth

Putting God First

Life in Christ is a journey of faith, transformation, and prioritization. As believers, we are chosen and created anew by God. He has called us to be a new creation, living a life where He holds the highest place. Our first and foremost priority in life must always be God. When we put Him first, He never allows us to remain last; rather, He exalts us and places us in positions of honor.

Chosen by God and Made a New Creation -God has chosen us to be His own, molding us in His image and renewing us through His grace. As a new creation in Christ, we are no longer bound by our past but are given a fresh start to walk in His ways. This transformation requires a shift in our priorities—placing God above everything else.

Give God Your First and Best-The principle of putting God first is essential. Our first moments of the day, our best energy, and our undivided attention should be dedicated to Him. Many times, people give God their leftover time— only after they have completed their daily routines. However, true devotion means setting aside the best part of our day for Him.

When we wake up in the morning, our first thoughts should be directed toward Him. Instead of rushing into the busyness of life, we must pause and spend quality time in His presence. This is not just about fulfilling a religious obligation but about developing an intimate relationship with Him. When we seek Him first, everything else falls into place.

God Never Leaves You Behind-One undeniable truth is that when we make God our priority, He makes us His priority. He never allows His children to fall behind. Instead, He leads, guides, and blesses them in every aspect of life. By surrendering our time, efforts, and plans to Him, we allow Him to work in ways beyond our imagination.

The Blessing of Quality Time with God-It is not just about spending time with God, but about giving Him our special and quality time. Sitting in His presence, meditating on His Word, and seeking His will should be our heart's desire. This intimate communion with Him strengthens our faith, brings peace to our hearts, and aligns our steps with His divine plan.

A Life Transformed by Prioritizing God-When we put God first, He takes care of everything else. He removes obstacles, opens doors, and ensures our path is directed according to His purpose. By making Him our ultimate priority, we experience His abundant grace and favor in every area of our lives.

Life in Christ is about devotion, commitment, and prioritization. Putting God first is not a one-time decision but a daily practice. When we seek Him before anything else, He aligns our lives with His will and blesses us beyond measure. May we always remember to give Him our first and best, for in doing so, we find true fulfillment, joy, and divine favor.

The Last Shall Be First

Do not worry about who has moved ahead of you. Do not dwell on thoughts like, "They have achieved more success," "They have worked more," "They are settled now, while I am still struggling," or "I have accomplished nothing yet." These thoughts are distractions that only bring stress and doubt.

Remember the promise written in the scriptures: The last shall be first. God knows how to uplift those who seem to be behind. He has the power to make the last one the most honored, the most successful, and the most blessed. Your journey is in His hands, and He has a perfect plan for you. Instead of worrying about who is ahead, celebrate the progress of others. Rejoice in their achievements, knowing that your time will come. Do not compare yourself to anyone, for everyone has a different path, a different timing, and a different purpose.

Stay at peace and remain tension-free. Keep walking with faith, knowing that when the right time comes, He will make you the greatest. Your destiny is secure in His hands, and He will ensure that you reach the heights meant for you. Trust in His divine order and continue forward with confidence, for He will make you the best in His perfect way and time.

My Testimony - Stay Strong in Practical Life

In life, there are moments when everything seems uncertain, when things don't go as planned, and when you feel like you're at the edge. But I want to share with you a truth that has carried me through the darkest times: when you remain strong in your practical life, your testimony becomes powerful. The more you stay grounded and firm in your actions, the louder your testimony speaks for you. I've learned that when you remain solid, you radiate strength. Even in the toughest situations, don't let yourself feel down. Always stand strong, no matter the challenges. Remember, you are the light of the world. You are like a rock that cannot be shaken. That is the essence of living with unwavering faith and strength.

I want to share an experience from a time when things were not easy. My husband and I were living with my in-laws at that time. It was their house, and we didn't have any authority to make decisions about anything. Their house, their vehicles – a car, a bike, a scooty – all belonged to them. I had to go to work every day, and we used their vehicle to commute. But one day, they decided to stop lending us their vehicle.

My husband was caught in a tough spot. He said, "I'm their son, and I don't even have the right to ask for this." I told him that we wouldn't argue or fight about it. We had to find a way, but there was no point in wasting time on a dispute. One early morning at 5 am, my father-in-law came to us and asked for the keys to the bike. I turned to my husband

and said, "Give it to him. It's alright. I'll take public transport to the office."

But deep down, I knew I had to pray. I asked God for a way, I asked for a vehicle of our own. At that time, we didn't have any savings or funds. Our bank balance was close to nothing. But I made a firm declaration in my heart. I said, "By the end of the day, we will have our own vehicle." I declared it with conviction, trusting that God would provide. I didn't just speak these words; I believed in them. That day, I went to the office by bus, not letting the situation hold me back. But I didn't lose my faith. In the evening, when I finished work, my husband and I went to a showroom to look at bikes. We didn't have much money, but we were determined to make it happen. We initially thought we would settle for an affordable, ordinary bike. However, the bike that caught our eye was much more expensive – around 2.5 to 3 lakh.

Some might have doubted. We didn't have the money. But I trusted God, and that night, by 5 pm, we had completed the documentation for our new bike. And by the end of the day, we brought our new bike home.

Looking back, we didn't have anything at that moment. But we had faith, and we had God with us. When God is by your side, nothing is impossible. It was not just a material victory; it was a testimony of God's provision and faithfulness.

I want to encourage you with this: stay strong in your practical life. **Don't let your bank balance define your worth**. It doesn't matter what you have or don't have.

When you have God on your side, everything will fall into place. That's the real strength. When you stay strong, no matter what, your testimony will speak for itself. Trust in God's timing, and watch as He turns your struggles into blessings.

Stay strong, stay grounded, and always keep your faith. God has a way of making everything work when you trust Him completely

My Testimony About Practical Faith

In my journey, I've come to realize that practical faith is key. Whenever I find myself in need of something, whether it's a material possession or a breakthrough in life, I don't sit and wait for things to happen. Instead, I start acting as if what I need is already in my hands, knowing that God will provide. This is how I live my life – with practical faith.

For example, there was a time when my husband and I needed a car. Instead of just waiting and wondering how it would happen, I started acting as if we already had it. Every day, without fail, I would tell my husband to park the car inside the courtyard, even though we didn't own one yet. It may seem small, but it was a declaration of faith. Every night when he locked the outer gate, I would say, "Park the car inside the courtyard." This was my practical way of showing belief that God would provide.

The months passed, and as December approached, I really desired to buy a new car. I continued with my daily practice, and then something interesting happened. My husband's birthday falls on December 31st, and jokingly, he asked me, "What are you going to gift me for my birthday this year?" I looked at him and said, "This time, the gift will come from God. It's going to be the best one."

And that's exactly what happened. God placed a thought in my heart. We decided to go to a showroom, and I told my husband to book the car. When we arrived, the salesman told us that it would take about a week for the car to be delivered. But in my heart, I believed that the car had to be delivered on my husband's birthday, December 31st. I believed it with all my heart.

On the morning of my husband's birthday, I told him to get ready and go to the showroom. He went, and when he arrived, the showroom told him it would take a little more time. But I had already placed everything in God's hands, knowing that He is faithful. And then, at 6:30 PM on the very same day, we received the delivery of our new car.

This was not just a coincidence. It was a testament to the power of practical faith. I held on to my expectation with unwavering strength, trusting that what God had promised would come to pass. The journey of believing and acting as if things were already in place worked wonders for us.

The key lesson here is this: when you have faith, back it up with action. Stay strong and keep your hopes alive. Trust that the one who promised is faithful. Don't let doubt or uncertainty shake your belief. Whatever you desire, start living as though you already have it. Keep your hands steady on the promises God has given you. The results will follow.

When you believe and act on your faith, miracles unfold in your life. Stay strong, stay practical, and keep holding on to your expectations. God is faithful, and He will always come through.

God's Promises Are Greater Than Our Requests

In life, there are moments when we ask God for something, thinking it's the best thing we could possibly receive. We pray, we ask, we plead – but little do we know, God's plans for us are always much bigger than what we can imagine. Sometimes, the things we ask for are small compared to what God is ready to give us. His promises, His blessings, are far beyond the limits of our understanding. What we request is only a glimpse of the miracles He is ready to unfold in our lives.

The Bible teaches us that God's Word is not just words on a page, but it is powerful and alive. His Word is sharper than any two-edged sword. It cuts through everything, distinguishing between what is true and false, right and wrong. God's Word is not bound by our limited understanding; it is alive and moving, transforming lives in ways we can't even imagine.

When we face battles in life, we must remember that we don't fight them with our own wisdom or strength. We fight with God's Word. It is the ultimate weapon, sharper than any sword, capable of piercing the deepest parts of our being. We don't have to rely on our own plans or strategies; we rely on God's Word, which is living and powerful.

One of the most beautiful aspects of God is that He speaks things into existence. When God says something, it happens. He calls things that are not as though they are, and that's the kind of faith we are to have. He doesn't speak based on the current circumstances or the limitations we see. He speaks with divine authority, and His words create miracles.

Sometimes, the thoughts and desires that come to our minds seem small and insignificant. We might think we are asking for something good, but God's vision for us is so much greater. What we think we need or want is only a fraction of the blessing He wants to pour out on us. His miracles go beyond our imaginations. What God can do is so much more than we could ever dream up ourselves.

It reminds me of how many times in my life I've asked for something, not knowing that God was preparing something far more wonderful. I've asked for small things, and God has given me far greater blessings. His miracles exceed our expectations and lead us to places we could never have reached on our own.

When you are in need, don't just ask for what you think is best. Trust that God knows what you need before you even ask. And when you speak, declare God's promises over your life with faith. His Word is alive, it's powerful, and it will not return void. It will accomplish what it was sent to do.

So, never underestimate the power of God's Word. Never think that what you are asking for is the limit of what God can do. Trust that when He speaks, it is always for your good, and His plans for you are far greater than anything you could ask for or imagine.

God is in the business of miracles. His Word, sharper than any sword, is the key to unlocking the abundant life He has promised us. When you stand on His promises, you can be sure that He will bring to pass everything He has spoken, and more. Always remember, what God gives is always greater than what we could ever imagine.

The Power of Faith in God's Word

In life, there are moments when everything seems uncertain, and the pressure of expectations weighs heavy. But as a believer, there is a profound truth that I stand by — whatever we say, it happens. Not just by chance, but because we are made in His image. We are the embodiment of Christ on Earth, and the words that come from us carry His divine power. I have experienced this truth in my life time and time again, and today I share with you the practical testimonies that confirm this power.

There was a time at my office when some of the employees were incredibly worried. They had been called into a meeting by the director, and the news they had was not good. They were afraid because the task they were given hadn't been completed as expected. They were sure they would be scolded or worse. The nervous energy in the air was palpable.

I overheard their conversation and, without thinking much, I asked them what was wrong. They explained their concerns, almost frantic in their worry. They were bracing themselves for the worst outcome. It was then that I simply said, "Nothing will happen. Trust God, everything will be fine." They looked at me, not quite convinced, and said, "You don't understand. They are really frustrated, and we haven't done what was expected." But I repeated, "Trust God. Nothing will happen. Believe me."

I could feel their doubt, but I stood firm in my faith. I told them, "If nothing happens, I will bet on it. They won't say anything negative. Just trust." The next day, after the meeting, I asked them how it went. They replied, "Nothing happened. They didn't say a word!" They were in shock. This was the same director who usually had a lot to say when things didn't go right. But that day, he remained silent. A miracle had happened.

In moments like these, I remind myself that we are made in God's image. As His children, our words have power. Just like Christ spoke and things happened, we too can speak and see things change. I have witnessed this in my life repeatedly, and I am certain that when we align ourselves with God's will, miracles unfold.

There was another instance when my team was under a lot of pressure about an upcoming review meeting. They called me late at night, anxious about what was going to happen. I could feel their stress even through the phone. But I simply told them, "Relax, everything is going to be fine. Don't worry about it." The next day, when the meeting took place, everything went smoothly, just as I had spoken. The topics discussed were exactly the ones I had mentioned the night before.

This is not just coincidence; this is the power of being in Christ. When we accept that He lives within us, that we are His body, the words we speak carry His authority. Just as He spoke and the world came into being, when we speak in

His name, we can change circumstances. Whatever we declare will come to pass. It's a principle that works because we are in Him and He is in us.

So, whenever you find yourself in a situation where things seem bleak or uncertain, remember: Trust God, speak with faith, and believe. You are His representative on Earth. What you speak in His name, with full assurance, will happen. We are not just anyone; we are His children, created in His image, and we carry the same authority. Speak life, speak blessings, and trust that He will make it happen, just as He always has

Rejoicing in the Lord, No Matter the Circumstances

"Rejoice in the Lord always; I will say it again: Rejoice!" – Philippians 4:4

This verse has been a guiding light in my life, especially when it comes to dealing with stress, anxiety, and worries. The Bible doesn't just ask us to be joyful in the good times, but to rejoice always, regardless of the situation. And the more I have meditated on this verse, the more I have realized the importance of letting go of my burdens and choosing joy.

There was a time when I found myself drowning in expenses. I began to meticulously track every cost, listing down where every penny was going. The list grew longer and longer, and with each line, the burden on my heart grew heavier. I found myself worrying, "How can I manage all of this? Where will all this money go? It feels like the expenses are never-ending, and I can't keep up with them."

But then, I remembered the Word of God. I recalled a scripture I had read in the Bible that spoke about giving our burdens to the Lord. It said, "Cast all your anxiety on Him because He cares for you" (1 Peter 5:7). I realized that this was a clear message for me — I was trying to carry the weight of all my financial worries when God had promised to take care of me. His Word assured me that He knows my needs and will provide for me in every situation.

So, I closed my diary, where I had been tracking all my expenses. I took a deep breath and said, "God, I give all of this to You. I know You can handle it much better than I ever could. I don't want to carry this burden anymore. Please take care of it and make everything easier for me. I trust You as my provider. I don't need to worry."

From that moment on, I stopped trying to keep track of every single expense. I stopped worrying about the future. I simply trusted God and released all the anxiety into His hands. I also reminded myself of what the Lord had said in His Word: "Rejoice in the Lord always." Even though my circumstances didn't immediately change, my heart shifted. I chose joy over worry. I chose peace over anxiety. I said to God, "You are the head of my house. You are the provider of everything I need. You gave me life, and I trust that You will fulfill every need I have. I don't have to worry about how things will work out because You are in control." And from that point on, I let go of the tension and the stress. I didn't allow myself to be consumed by worries anymore. Instead, I chose to focus on the goodness of God and trust that He would take care of everything. I decided to rejoice in the Lord, just as He instructed.

As time went on, I saw God's provision in ways I had never imagined. I realized that the peace and joy that came from surrendering my worries to Him were worth far more than any material thing I could have gained by stressing over the situation. God's provision is not just financial; it's emotional, spiritual, and relational. When we trust Him, He truly does make all things work together for good.

So, every time I faced a challenge, I reminded myself of this: "Rejoice in the Lord always!" No matter what life throws at me, I choose joy. I choose to cast all my cares upon Him and trust that He will take care of everything. And every time I do this, I experience the freedom that comes from knowing that God is my provider and that I don't need to worry

God Will Supply All Your Needs

"And my God will meet all your needs according to the riches of His glory in Christ Jesus." – Philippians 4:19

This verse holds a powerful promise for every believer: God will supply all our needs. And I've seen this truth come alive in my own life, not just in theory but in the most practical way.

There was a time when I found myself in a very difficult financial situation. I had no job, no income, and honestly, not much hope either. It was a time when everything seemed uncertain, and the stress of financial instability was heavy on my heart. But one thing I held onto firmly was my trust in God. I knew that He was my provider, and that I could depend on Him.

At that time, I had learned about tithing. I had heard that tithing is like planting a seed. It's not just about money, but it's about giving something that honors God. I understood that tithing could be in many forms—not just money, but also any work or action that brings glory to God. It was a principle of faith and trust.

One day, I found that I had only 60 rupees left in my purse. It wasn't much, but I knew I had to give it. I decided that this 60 rupees would be my tithe, and I would honor God with it. I didn't have much to give, but I had a heart full of trust. I didn't say a long prayer; I just gave it in faith, knowing that God would honor my obedience.

In that moment, I didn't know how or when things would change, but I believed God would come through. A few days later, an opportunity opened up, and I was offered a job. The salary was 65,000 rupees—a huge blessing for me at the time! I couldn't believe it. It was so much more than I had expected.

When I reflected on what had happened, I remembered that simple act of faith. I had trusted God with what little I had, and He had multiplied it. This experience taught me that God doesn't require us to give out of our abundance, but out of faith. When we honor Him, even with a small amount, He is faithful to provide for us.

God's provision is not limited to money; it extends to every area of our lives. When we put our trust in Him and take steps of faith, He meets our needs in ways we could never have imagined. I also learned that tithing is not about expecting something in return; it's about showing love and obedience to God. It's about honoring Him with whatever we have, knowing that He is the source of everything.

Tithing isn't a transaction where we give to get. It's an act of faith and love, showing God that we trust Him to provide for us. When we give, we demonstrate that we believe He is our ultimate provider, and that He will supply all our needs. That's the beauty of tithing—it's not just about finances, it's about trusting God with everything in our lives.

I've come to realize that God always provides when we trust Him. His timing is perfect, and His ways are greater than ours. He is faithful to meet all our needs, whether big or small, and His provision is a testimony of His goodness and love. As we give, we don't give out of obligation, but out of love for the One who provides everything we need. And when we do, we experience His faithfulness in the most practical ways.

God's promise to meet our needs is true, and I have witnessed it in my own life. When we honor Him, He honors us. And that's why I can confidently say that God will supply all your needs, just as He did for me, and He will do so in a way that will leave you in awe of His love and provision

The Promise of Provision

In Psalm 81:10, God reassures us: "I am the Lord your God, who brought you out of the land of Egypt; open your mouth wide, and I will fill it." This verse speaks to the unwavering faithfulness of God and His promise to provide for His people in every circumstance.

When God led us out of the wilderness, we faced a time when there was no place to call our own. It seemed as if the path ahead was uncertain, and the resources to sustain us were scarce. But God's promise was true. He did not bring us this far to leave us in need. He guided us, prepared everything, and provided for every single need. What seemed like a barren place, devoid of provision, was transformed by His faithfulness.

Think of Abraham, who, when he had nothing—no land, no wealth—spoke of fields, flocks, and blessings. He trusted God's word, and despite the seeming lack, he received abundance. God provided everything, even when it looked impossible. When God promises, He does not fail. From nothing, He brings forth everything.

God's promises are not dependent on our circumstances. When we face challenges or feel like we are walking through dry lands, it is a time to trust that the same God who brought us out of difficult situations will continue to provide.

"Ask, and it shall be given to you." Whatever you need, God is already ahead of you, preparing the way. His provision is certain, and He will not leave you lacking. The same God who brought you out of the wilderness is the One who will give you everything you need. So, do not fear. Trust in His provision, for He will fill your life abundantly, just as He promised.

In every trial, in every situation, God is with you. He has always been faithful, and He will continue to be. The story of Abraham, the story of the Israelites, and the story of our lives is a testament to the unfailing provision of the Lord. Whatever you need, ask, and it will be given. Hold firm to His promises—He will never leave you without.

The Assurance of God's Provision

In 1 Corinthians 1:7, we are given a powerful promise: "So that you do not lack any spiritual gift as you eagerly wait for our Lord Jesus Christ to be revealed." This verse assures us that God, in His infinite grace, has already equipped us with everything we need.

The promises of God are not vague or uncertain; they are written and guaranteed. The Apostle Paul reminds us that when God provides, He does so fully. There will be no lack in any area of our lives, especially when it comes to the blessings and spiritual gifts that God has given us. His provision is abundant and complete, and it is not dependent on our circumstances or efforts. We don't have to struggle or strive excessively to receive what God has already promised.

Many times, we may feel as if we are lacking something—whether it's strength, wisdom, or peace. But the truth is, God has already provided for all our needs. There is no area of our lives where we are truly without. When we look to Him, we realize that His promises are written, and they cannot fail. We don't need to work endlessly, fighting for every small piece. His provision is already prepared for us. Imagine being in a race, where the finish line is already set, and all that is left for you to do is walk towards it. This is the picture of our walk with God. We don't need to fight for the gifts or blessings He has already placed before us. We simply need to trust Him and remain faithful. His promise assures us that we won't lack anything we need, especially when it comes to the spiritual and eternal gifts He has for us.

So, when life becomes difficult, or when we feel like we're in need, remember this promise: **There will be no lack**. God will not leave us wanting. His gifts are already given, and His provision is sure. We don't need to fret or worry. He has already provided for everything, and in His timing, we will see it unfold.

Trust in His written promises. No matter what comes your way, God's provision and grace will meet you exactly where you need it. Rest in the certainty that there is no shortage in God's economy.

The Power of Words

In Ephesians 4:29, we are reminded of a crucial principle: *"Do not let any unwholesome talk come out of your mouths, but only what is helpful for building others up according to their needs, that it may benefit those who listen."* This verse highlights the importance of the words we speak and the power they hold.

In the past, many of us may have spoken without thinking, letting words slip out that were harsh, unkind, or careless. But now, as followers of Christ, we are called to be mindful of what we say. Our words should not only reflect our own growth but also contribute to the growth of others. Each word we speak has the potential to either build someone up or tear them down.

The Bible teaches us that our speech is not just a casual matter—it carries weight. Our words have the power to bring life or death, encouragement or discouragement, peace or conflict. When we speak, we release power. And when we speak with love, grace, and truth, that power is used for good.

Now, more than ever, we must be careful with our words. They should always be positive, uplifting, and beneficial for the well-being of others. Our words should reflect the character of Christ, speaking with wisdom and love. If we are truly seeking to bless others, we must choose to speak words that build others up, words that encourage, words that strengthen their faith and character.

We must remember that our words are not only for our own benefit but also for the benefit of those who hear us. Whether at work, at home, or in our communities, the things we say can either encourage someone in their walk with God or discourage them. Our words should reflect the heart of God—a heart that desires to bless and to build, not to harm or destroy.

Blessings—that is what we should speak over others. Speak life into the lives of those around you. Speak words that inspire, words that bring peace, words that give hope. Let your speech be filled with kindness and compassion, because what we say has the power to shape the lives of others.

So, let us choose our words wisely. Let them be words of encouragement, love, and grace. And in doing so, we will not only bless others, but we will also see the power of God at work in our own lives.

Everything Works for My Good

There's a powerful truth that I've learned over time: **everything works together for my good**. No matter what happens, I now believe that every situation, even the challenging ones, is ultimately for my benefit. No one can harm me in the way I once feared because I know that God is in control, and He is always working things out for me.

There was a time when I had a clear plan for my life. After getting married, I thought my next step would be to move abroad with my husband. I had everything ready—the paperwork, the plans, the excitement. But, as life often goes, circumstances changed in a way I never expected. At that time, it seemed frustrating, even discouraging. I didn't understand why things weren't going according to plan. But looking back now, I can see that those situations weren't mistakes or setbacks—they were a part of God's perfect plan. If those events hadn't happened, I wouldn't have grown as close to God as I did. It was through those challenges that I learned to lean on Him in ways I never had before.

I realized that sometimes, when things don't go as we expect, it's because God has a better plan—one that draws us closer to Him. Just like a child who seeks comfort from their mother when they're sick, we, too, need to seek God's presence when we are hurting or confused. Just as a mother cares for her child, God cares for us, and sometimes, He allows us to go through difficulties so that we can experience His love and care more intimately.

There were times when we were alone, facing challenges that seemed too big to handle. There were moments when I would cry, wondering why everything was happening to us. But in those moments, God was closer than ever. His presence became my comfort. I would go into my room, pour out my heart to Him, and feel His peace wash over me. In the silence of those moments, I realized that material things—money, cars, houses—are just that: things. They come and go. But a relationship with God? That's something that stays, something that only grows stronger the more we experience His presence.

I used to think that success and happiness were tied to external things. But now I understand that true joy comes from being close to God. The more I sought Him, the more I realized that nothing else could satisfy in the way His presence did. When others spoke negatively about us, we didn't respond in anger. Instead, we would retreat to our private space and talk to God. We found solace in His presence, and over time, we learned to trust Him even more.

What I've learned is that everything—good and bad— works together for my benefit. Even when things don't go the way I planned, I know God is using it to shape me, to bring me closer to Him, and to prepare me for something even better. When you experience God in a deep, personal way, everything else fades in comparison. The material things may come and go, but His love and presence will always remain, and that's where true peace and happiness lie.

So, whenever life seems to take an unexpected turn, remember: **it's all working for your good**. Keep trusting, keep seeking Him, and you'll find that even the most difficult moments can lead you to a deeper relationship with God

The Power of What You Focus On

If you want to live a peaceful and joyful life, one of the most important things you can do is stay away from hearsay and gossip. There's a lot of noise in the world around us—rumors, discussions, and news that only serve to fill our minds with unnecessary tension and stress. The things you see and hear affect your emotions, thoughts, and ultimately, your actions. This is why I've made a conscious decision to avoid certain things. For example, I don't watch the news anymore, because I realized that what you expose yourself to can have a strong impact on your heart and mind.

When you watch violent or disturbing content, it can stir up negative emotions, fear, and anxiety in your heart. These emotions may come and go, but they affect your peace of mind. It's easy to get caught up in the chaos of the world, especially when it's shared everywhere, but we have a choice in what we allow to enter our hearts and minds. If you see or hear something negative, especially on social media or through word of mouth, think twice about engaging in it. When we discuss these things with others, we are unknowingly spreading fear and negativity.

Instead of focusing on things that bring worry, why not spend that time with God? We have a limited amount of time in a day, and that time can either be spent on things that bring peace or on things that distract us from the peace God offers. Why not use that time to seek God, to explore His kingdom, and to grow closer to Him? The world around us can be full of distractions, but the time we spend with God is the most valuable. It's in those quiet moments with Him that we find true peace, wisdom, and clarity.

Jesus taught us to pray, "Our Father, who art in heaven, hallowed be Thy name. Thy kingdom come, Thy will be done, on earth as it is in heaven." If you desire to see His kingdom come to earth, then let's focus on spreading His kingdom values. We must align our words and actions with His will. What kind of world do you want to see? If we want peace, love, and righteousness to fill the earth, it starts with us—living those values and not being swayed by the chaos around us.

We are called to pray for God's kingdom to come and His will to be done on earth, just as it is in heaven. This means we have to live with intention—intentionally seeking peace, truth, and righteousness, and rejecting the negativity that the world offers.

If you desire His kingdom, then actively participate in it. Turn away from things that bring harm and embrace those that bring life. Speak life into situations, spread love, and stand firm in His peace. Our minds are precious, and what we fill them with shapes how we live. So, let's choose to fill our minds with what is pure, lovely, and of good report, as the Bible says, and reject anything that disturbs our inner peace.

In the end, it's all about perspective. What we focus on shapes our lives. If you want peace and happiness, then focus on God and His kingdom, not on the noise and negativity that surrounds us. And as we do this, we will not only experience peace but will become instruments of peace in the world around us

God's Provision for the Righteous

In Proverbs 10:3, we find a comforting promise: *"The Lord does not let the righteous go hungry."* This verse speaks to the faithfulness of God to provide for those who live according to His ways. It reminds us that when we walk in righteousness, God is our provider and protector. He will not allow us to be in want or lack what we need.

This promise is not just about physical hunger; it encompasses every area of our lives. The righteous are those who seek to live in alignment with God's will, and when we do so, we can trust that He will take care of our needs. The verse assures us that even in difficult times, God will provide for us, and we will not be left to suffer needlessly.

Sometimes, life may present challenges that make us feel uncertain about the future. We might face moments when resources seem scarce, or the way ahead feels unclear. In those moments, it's easy to become anxious or worried. However, God reminds us that His provision is not dependent on the world's circumstances, but on His faithful nature. Just as a good parent makes sure their child has what they need, our Heavenly Father ensures that we lack nothing essential.

In the context of this proverb, the righteous person is not just someone who behaves well or follows the rules; it's someone who trusts in God's provision and acts in faith. This trust leads to peace, knowing that our Heavenly Father is aware of our needs and will take care of them in His perfect timing. We do not have to chase after material things in desperation, for God knows what we need and promises to provide for us.

It's important to recognize that God's provision may not always look like what we expect. His ways are higher than ours, and sometimes He provides in unexpected ways. Just as God provided for the Israelites in the wilderness with manna and quail, He will provide for us in ways that might surprise us. His provision is always for our good, and often, He uses times of difficulty to draw us closer to Him, teaching us to rely on Him fully.

This verse also speaks to the character of God. He is not a distant or uncaring Father. He sees the needs of His people, and He is faithful to provide for them. In our world, where scarcity and fear of lack often dominate, we can take comfort in knowing that our God is abundant in love and provision.

As believers, we are called to trust in God's goodness and faithfulness. When we live with righteousness in our hearts and trust in His promises, we can rest assured that He will never let us go hungry. Whether it's physical sustenance, emotional support, or spiritual nourishment, God will provide for us every step of the way.

So, whenever you find yourself in need or struggling with uncertainty, remember the promise of Proverbs 10:3. God will not allow the righteous to go hungry. Trust in His provision, and be assured that He will meet your needs, just as He always has and always will

‘My Practical’s

When we first moved into our new house, it was semi-furnished. At that time, we didn't have a lot of things, but there was always this dream of turning it into a proper home. I remember thinking about how everything would come together. We had the basics, but there were still so many things missing—things that would make the house truly ours.

A few days after moving in, I realized that there were a few essentials we needed urgently: a water purifier, a refrigerator, a washing machine, an inverter, a sofa couch, a geyser, a blower, and more. At first, I didn't really stress about it. I would just stand in different rooms and imagine how everything would fit. I would say to myself, "The sofa will go here," and in the kitchen, "The refrigerator will be placed right here." Walking into the bathroom, I'd picture the washing machine in place. Even the empty spaces didn't feel empty for long. I kept saying to myself, "Soon, this will be taken care of."

And before I knew it, one by one, everything we needed started arriving. It was like magic. I didn't have to worry about how it would all work out. Things just started falling into place, as if by some unseen hand.

It wasn't just about getting the things we needed. It was about trusting that everything would come together at the right time. And I truly believe it was God's grace that made it all happen. I've always prayed for His help, and I've realized that with faith, everything works out in the end. Sometimes, things don't happen exactly how you imagine, but as long as you trust the process, everything will be okay.

Looking back, I see how everything we needed came together so seamlessly. What started as just a house turned into a home, and for that, I am deeply thankful. It reminded me that sometimes, it's not just the practical steps we take that matter, but the faith and patience we have in the process

The Dream of the Studio

My husband had always dreamed of opening a music studio. He had this vision, this passion, but at that time, we didn't have the resources. There was nothing, and the idea of starting something so big seemed almost impossible. But then, something happened. One day, it was like a spark of faith was placed in my heart. I felt strongly that I should start talking about the studio, even if we didn't have anything yet. It felt like God was guiding me, telling me to take that first step.

So, I began speaking about it, saying that we would have a studio. I found an old table lying around the house, and I brought it into the room, setting it up as if it was already part of the studio. I stood in front of it, praying with all my heart, thanking God for the studio we were going to have. I made it a habit to speak it every day, declaring that the studio was coming into existence.

My husband would often say, "It's going to cost a lot. The equipment is expensive." But I would reassure him, saying, "For us, nothing is expensive. Everything is affordable. We get everything from heaven, and God will arrange everything for us." I knew deep down that we were in the hands of a loving Father who would provide for us, and I trusted that with all my heart.

And before we knew it, the studio started taking shape. Everything we needed, one by one, came together. The equipment, the space, the setup—everything. It was like a dream that was being slowly built, piece by piece, and every day I could see it becoming a reality.

In the end, the studio was ready, and it was everything we had hoped for. All the doubts and worries about cost or how we would manage were gone. We realized that with faith, and with God by our side, nothing was impossible. The studio didn't just come together with hard work; it came together because we believed in it and trusted that God would take care of the rest.

It was a beautiful reminder that when you put your faith in Him, everything you need will be provided, and dreams will come true.

Strength through Faith- Practical

God has made me so strong that there is never any fear in my heart. No matter what challenges come my way, I never worry about what's next or how life will unfold. There was a time when we were told to leave our home, and everyone around us might have been anxious, but I felt no fear. I didn't worry. I knew we would be fine.

I always say that there is victory in my name. I can never lose. God has given me the spirit of victory, and because of that, I walk through life with the confidence that no matter what comes my way, I will overcome. We are people who have already won, who are victorious. Fear is not part of our mindset. We always carry a "win-win" attitude.

Our teacher, Jesus, already conquered death itself. He won the greatest battle, and if He can conquer death, then there is nothing in this world—no challenge, no small problem—that can shake us. We are more than conquerors. This world's little issues, situations, or troubles are nothing at all compared to the victory we have in Him.

With this belief, I walk through life without fear. No matter what the future holds or where we have to go, I know that God is with us, guiding us, and giving us the strength to overcome anything. Life might have its twists and turns, but with God on our side, we can never be defeated. The victory is already ours.

"Come to Me, All Who Labor and Are Heavy Laden, and I Will Give You Peace"

In the hustle and bustle of life, many find themselves burdened by the weight of the world. It is said in the scriptures, "Come to me, all who labor and are heavy laden, and I will give you peace." These words hold a profound truth, reminding us that amidst life's struggles, there is a source of solace and comfort — a divine peace that transcends all troubles.

 (God offers us His peace in this world, yet often, it is we who allow ourselves to be overwhelmed by worry, sorrow, and pain. We carry burdens that were never meant to be ours. Each day, we place heavy loads upon our shoulders — responsibilities, fears, anxieties — but we forget to turn to the One who is capable of lightening our load. He asks us to lay down our burdens at His feet, for He is the caretaker who watches over us.

In the chaos of life, many forget that the weight they bear is not theirs to carry alone. When we continue to hold onto our worries and fears, we don't give God the opportunity to work in our lives. We try to control everything, to manage every aspect of our existence, but in doing so, we end up exhausting ourselves, both physically and mentally.

A beautiful story comes to mind. Once, a person came to me for an interview. This person was working night shifts and was struggling with managing his responsibilities. When I asked him how he managed the day shift and the night shift together, his answer struck me deeply. He said,

"The responsibilities don't let me sleep." His words made me realize how many people in this world torture themselves, pushing their limits, believing they must carry everything on their own.

But that is not what GOD wants for us. He doesn't want us to live under such a heavy burden. He desires for us to live a life of peace, of joy. He never intended for us to carry so much suffering. It is often humans who trap themselves in their own struggles, forgetting that the true source of peace is in surrendering to God's will. When we carry the burden of life alone, we distance ourselves from the peace that Parmeshwar offers us.

God's gifts are free from sorrow. The wealth He provides does not come with the weight of pain and hardship. It is we, through our actions and choices, who allow ourselves to be trapped in the cycle of worry and suffering. But Parmeshwar's promise is clear: if we come to Him, if we lay down our burdens, He will give us peace — a peace that surpasses understanding, a peace that heals.

In the midst of life's struggles, let us remember to turn to Him, to trust in His care. Let us lay down our worries and find comfort in His embrace. For He has given us the greatest gift of all — His Son, that we may live a life of joy, free from the weight of unnecessary burdens.

Let go of the pain, the stress, the worry, and simply *experience* His peace.

"The Power of Persistence and Faith"

There are times in life when it feels like everything is against us. The challenges seem endless, and it's hard to figure out how to manage it all. We often find ourselves asking, "How will I handle this? Where will the resources come from? Why isn't anything working out?" It's in these moments of doubt and frustration that we need to remember something important — *the power of persistence and faith*.

Imagine this: when we work out, especially in the beginning, it feels like nothing is changing. The results aren't immediate, the muscles aren't showing up right away, and we wonder if all the effort is even worth it. At first, when we start warming up, it feels like we can't go on, like we're pushing ourselves too hard. But the real transformation happens after that — once the actual workout begins, that's when the muscles start to grow. It's not always instant, but through consistent effort, those curves, that shape, start to appear.

Life is very much the same. In the face of struggles, when nothing seems to be working, it's easy to become discouraged. But just like with exercise, real growth doesn't always happen at first sight. The results come after consistent effort and belief. We have to keep pushing through, even when it feels like we're not getting anywhere.

The key is to stay constant in your faith. When you believe, truly believe, that things will work out, even in the darkest moments, you open the door to transformation. Even though situations may seem overwhelming, remember, it's often right at the edge of those hardest moments that the breakthrough happens.

It's when you feel like you can't take it anymore, that's when the real growth is beginning to take shape.
In moments of doubt, remember that just like the muscles developing in a workout, the results of your hard work — in faith, in effort, in perseverance — are coming. They may not be visible right away, but keep going. Keep trusting. Believe that your efforts are not in vain. Because just like with exercise, the breakthrough happens when you push through, when you don't give up.
So, if you're feeling lost or stuck, remember: *this too shall pass*. Stay in faith, remain consistent, and understand that the results will come. The work is happening, even if you can't see it yet. Trust the process, and you'll see that everything you've been working towards will eventually come together

"Trusting in God's Honor and Guidance"

Psalm 25:2 is a verse that speaks deeply to the heart of every believer: *"O my God, I trust in You; let me not be ashamed; let not my enemies triumph over me."* These words are a beautiful reminder of the unwavering trust we are called to place in God, and the honor and dignity He grants us as we follow Him.

There are many times in life when we feel vulnerable, when situations seem out of our control, and the weight of fear or shame threatens to overwhelm us. We may face challenges that make us question our worth or even our ability to succeed. We wonder if we will be ridiculed, if others will look down on us, or if we will be shamed for our actions or decisions. But this verse reminds us that when we place our trust in God, He shields us from such shame.

God's Honor in Our Lives

When we trust in God, we are never left to face our struggles alone. He does not allow us to be disgraced or humiliated in the face of adversity. The verse tells us that we will not be ashamed, meaning God upholds our dignity and guides us with wisdom and strength. No matter the circumstances or the difficulties we face, when we rely on Him, He ensures that our integrity is protected and that we are never reduced to a state of shame.

In fact, God does the opposite. He lifts us up. He gives us honor even in the most challenging situations. We don't need to compromise our values or integrity to find success or approval. With God by our side, every task we undertake becomes an opportunity to reflect His grace and His honor. God, in His infinite mercy, ensures that those who trust in Him are treated with respect and are given strength to overcome the obstacles they face.

A Life of Dignity and Strength

What does it mean to live without shame and with honor? It means that even when others may mock, criticize, or challenge us, we remain steadfast in our faith. It means we don't allow fear or insecurity to dictate our actions. We are not ruled by the opinions of others, but by the assurance that God's presence in our lives gives us the dignity we need to walk with our heads held high.

God does not just protect us from shame; He empowers us to walk in confidence. We are never asked to bow down in humility before the troubles of this world. Instead, we are given the courage to stand tall, knowing that God honors those who trust in Him. Our actions are infused with His grace, and the results, even if not immediately visible, will always reflect His goodness.

The Power of Trust

Psalm 25:2 calls us to trust in God wholeheartedly. When we do so, we are assured that we will not be put to shame. This trust isn't about denying challenges or ignoring difficulties. It's about understanding that with God's guidance, no matter what happens, we will walk in His strength, not in weakness. And when we are grounded in His honor, our actions reflect His goodness to the world around us.

It's important to remember that trusting in God means letting go of the need to control everything. It means surrendering our fears and anxieties into His hands, knowing He will direct our paths. When we trust Him, He makes sure that we are always treated with respect and honor, even in the midst of life's trials.

In moments of doubt, remember that God will never allow you to be put to shame. Trust in Him, and He will elevate you, guide you, and keep you from harm. You will not be defeated. Instead, you will rise with honor, your head held high, and your heart full of His peace

"Blessings in Every Bite"

The Bible speaks to us in many ways, offering us wisdom and comfort in both big and small matters. One such verse that stands out is the promise that God will bless our food and heal our bodies: *"He will bless your bread and your water, and I will take away sickness from among you."* (Exodus 23:25). This verse is a reminder that when we trust in God, He not only provides for our needs but also protects and blesses the food we consume, making it a source of health and strength.

In today's world, where corruption and contamination seem to seep into every corner, it's easy to worry about what we are consuming. We hear about food being adulterated, markets filled with fake products, and every item we purchase being tampered with in some way. The question arises: can we trust what we eat? In the midst of these concerns, I realized something important. Though the world around us may be filled with deceit and contamination, we have a powerful tool — prayer.

I remember a time when I felt uncertain about the food we were receiving in our home. I'd heard so much about adulterated goods and how everything in the market seems to be mixed with something harmful. It was unsettling. But instead of letting this fear control me, I turned to prayer. I said to God, *"Lord, You know what we are eating, and I cannot speak for everything in the world. But I trust in Your power to make it pure. Whatever food or drink comes into our home, I ask that You bless it, purify it, and keep it free from any harmful substance. May everything we consume be natural, wholesome, and beneficial for our health. Let no impurity or contamination affect us. Protect us from anything that might harm us."*

When we speak God's name and trust in His power, He listens. And just as He has promised, He blesses the bread and water we take, transforming them into sources of nourishment and health. God is capable of purifying what is tainted and making it beneficial for our bodies. When we pray over our food, we invite His blessings to cover it — to remove any harmful additives, to ensure that what we are consuming is truly good for us.

This doesn't mean we should ignore the importance of being cautious about what we buy or eat, but it does remind us that ultimately, our health and well-being are in God's hands. God is able to protect us from the effects of poison or harmful substances. In a world full of uncertainty, His protection brings peace and assurance. As He says, *"I will take away sickness from among you."* This is not just a promise for the ancient Israelites but for all of us who trust in Him today.

When we take the time to pray over our meals, we are not only giving thanks but also acknowledging God's power to bless us. We are inviting His protection into our daily lives. The simple act of praying before eating becomes a declaration of faith — faith that God is with us, faith that He will keep us safe, and faith that He will bless what we consume, making it pure and life-giving.

As we say grace, we recognize that it is God who sustains us. It is His blessing that makes our food not only sufficient but nourishing for our bodies. With every bite, we remember that we are not alone in this world. God is watching over us, guiding us, and providing for us in ways we may not always see or understand, but His blessings are there, even in the simplest of things.

So, let us always give thanks for the food we receive. Let us pray over it, trusting that God will bless it, and may His grace cover every meal we partake in. For as Scripture reminds us, *"He will bless your bread and your water, and I will take away sickness from among you."* With God's blessings, we are assured of a healthy, peaceful life — free from harm, free from sickness, and filled with the abundance of His grace.

So, eat with gratitude, trusting that God is with you in every moment, ensuring that the nourishment you receive is pure, clean, and good for your health

"God Will Remove All Insults and Mockery"

Isaiah 25:8 declares a powerful promise from God: *"He will swallow up death forever, and the Sovereign Lord will wipe away the tears from all faces; He will remove His people's disgrace from all the earth. The Lord has spoken."* This verse brings a profound message of hope and assurance — God promises to remove all insults, mockery, and disgrace from our lives. No matter what others say or think, God will elevate us and protect our dignity. You don't need to worry about the opinions of others, because God's truth is greater than any judgment or insult thrown your way.

There are times in life when people may belittle you, mock your efforts, or even undermine your abilities. They may look at you and say, "What can you possibly do? You are nothing. You will never succeed." But in those moments, we must remember that *God's promise stands* — He will remove all those insults, and He will raise you up in His time. The very people who mock you today will one day see the glory of God in your life, and they will be the ones praising you.

It is easy to feel discouraged when others don't see your worth, but God sees you differently. He sees your potential, your strength, and your worth. The mockery and insults of today are temporary, but God's word is eternal. His promise is that He will lift you up and cause others to recognize your value.

I have a personal story to share that reflects this truth. There was a time when someone looked at me and said,

"What can this girl possibly achieve? Her department is a mess, and she'll never succeed." It was a harsh and discouraging comment. But I refused to accept that as my truth. I declared in my heart that God would remove those words and replace them with honor. I trusted that God had a plan for me, and He would give me the strength to overcome all obstacles.

Years passed, and the very people who once mocked me began to see the change. They saw the growth, the determination, and the respect I earned — not through my own efforts alone, but through the grace of God. Eventually, those same people who had belittled me began to speak differently. They started calling me "the pillar," saying, "She is the best. She has risen to the top, and we respect her." It was as if God had turned the tide, and what was once mockery turned into praise.

This is the power of God in action. He doesn't let us stay in our disgrace. He doesn't allow the insults of others to define us. Instead, He takes those insults and uses them as stepping stones to elevate us. When God is on your side, no one can hold you back. He is the one who truly gives honor, and He ensures that you never have to live under the weight of shame or humiliation.

God's promise is clear: He will not allow us to be ashamed or humiliated forever. The very people who mock us will one day recognize the grace and power of God in our lives. In the end, it is God who raises us up. He is our dignity, our protector, and our source of strength.

As Christians, we are called to live in the confidence that comes from knowing that *we are His* — we are His children, His beloved ones, and no one can take that away. When others insult or mock us, we don't need to react with bitterness or anger. Instead, we can turn to God, knowing that He will fight our battles and bring justice in His time.

As the Bible says, *"He will not let us be put to shame."* Whatever your circumstances, whatever insults or mockery you may face today, remember that they are temporary. God's plan for you is greater than any judgment from others. Keep trusting in Him, and in due time, He will lift you up and bring honor where there was once disgrace.

Never forget: You are a child of the Most High, and He will never let you stay in shame. He will always raise you up, and He will always protect your dignity. You are not defined by what others say; you are defined by what God has spoken over your life. And His word is that He will make you a pillar, a source of strength and honor, for His glory.

So, stand tall, and trust that the God who has spoken is faithful to bring to pass every word He has spoken about you.

"God's Unfailing Promise: I Will Never Leave You"

Hebrews 13:5 reminds us of one of the most comforting promises in Scripture: *"Never will I leave you; never will I forsake you."* This promise, spoken by God Himself, reassures us that no matter what we face in life, we are never alone. God's presence is constant, and His faithfulness is unshakeable. In every situation, in every storm, He will never leave us. His love and care for us are unchanging.

There are times in life when we may feel abandoned or forgotten. We might go through seasons of hardship, loneliness, or confusion, and it can feel as though we're facing the world by ourselves. We may wonder if anyone truly understands our struggles or if anyone will stand by us when things get tough. In these moments, it's important to remember that God's promise is true — He will never leave us or forsake us. He is always there, walking with us through every challenge and every trial.

God is not like humans. People may leave us, betray us, or disappoint us, but God's faithfulness remains. He doesn't promise that life will always be easy or without difficulty, but He does promise that He will be with us through it all. Whether we are on a mountaintop or in a valley, God is by our side. His presence is a constant source of strength, comfort, and peace.

I remember a time in my life when I felt overwhelmed by the weight of responsibilities and struggles. It seemed like

I was carrying more than I could handle. The challenges seemed insurmountable, and I began to question if I could go on. But in that moment of despair, I heard God's whisper in my heart: *"I will never leave you. I will never forsake you."* It was as if those words came straight from the depths of my soul, bringing peace and reassurance that no matter what, I was not alone. God was with me. And in that moment, I found the strength to keep going.

This is the beauty of God's promise — it's not just a distant hope, but a present reality. We are not abandoned to face life's challenges on our own. God is always with us, providing His support, His wisdom, and His strength. We may not always feel His presence, but the truth remains that He is faithful. When we feel weak, He is our strength. When we feel lost, He is our guide. When we feel afraid, He is our courage.

God promises that He will never let us be defeated. He will never allow us to face any situation without being there to help us through it. Even when the world seems to be falling apart, His presence remains steady. He will never let us fall beyond His reach. As we walk through life, we can rest in the assurance that we are not walking alone. God's hand is always extended toward us, ready to lift us up, to comfort us, and to lead us to victory.

In those moments when we feel like giving up, when the burden seems too heavy to carry, let us hold onto this promise: *God will never leave us.* No matter what we face, no matter how dark the day may seem, He is always with us. He is our rock, our refuge, and our strength. He will never abandon us, no matter how difficult the circumstances.

We must remind ourselves that God is faithful, even when we don't see the solution right away. His timing is perfect, and His ways are higher than our own. We may not always understand why we go through certain struggles, but we can trust that God is working all things together for our good. His promise to never leave us is unchanging, and He is always with us, guiding us through every trial and challenge.

So, whatever you may be going through today, know that God's promise is true: He will never leave you. He will never forsake you. You are never alone. Trust in His faithfulness and rest in the assurance that He is with you, every step of the way. He will give you the strength to face every challenge and the peace to overcome every fear. *You are not alone — God is with you.* And because of His promise, you will never be defeated

"God is Always with You: A Promise of Strength and Victory"

Deuteronomy 31:6 says: *"Be strong and courageous. Do not be afraid or terrified because of them, for the Lord your God goes with you; He will never leave you nor forsake you."* This verse is a powerful reminder that no matter what we face in life, God is with us. His presence is constant, His strength is unshakeable, and His promises are faithful. When we hold on to this truth, we can face any challenge with confidence, knowing that we will never fail because God is with us.

There are times in life when we feel uncertain, when we face difficulties that seem too big to overcome, and when the path ahead feels unclear. It is during these moments that we often wonder if we will succeed, if we will make it through, or if we are strong enough to endure. But Deuteronomy 31:6 gives us the assurance that God is always by our side. He is not a distant God; He walks with us every step of the way, guiding us, strengthening us, and supporting us.

When I reflect on this verse, it always reminds me that I am never alone in any situation. Whether it's at work, in relationships, or in personal challenges, I can trust that God is right there with me. This assurance lifts the weight of fear and doubt from my heart because I know that no matter how difficult the task may seem, God will never leave me to face it on my own. With God by my side, I can be strong and courageous, knowing that failure is not an option because He will help me succeed.

It's easy to become discouraged when things don't go as planned. There are times when we work hard and still don't see the results we expect. But the truth is, God's plans for us are always greater than our own. His purpose for our lives is always for good, and He will never leave us or forsake us in the midst of challenges. Even when we can't see the outcome, we can trust that God is working behind the scenes, leading us toward victory.

When I was going through a particularly tough season in my life, I felt overwhelmed by the challenges in front of me. There were so many uncertainties and obstacles, and it seemed like every step forward was met with resistance. But then I reminded myself of Deuteronomy 31:6. I held on to the truth that God was with me, that He would never leave me, and that He would help me through every difficulty. With that confidence, I began to face each day with renewed strength and courage. Slowly but surely, God opened doors, provided solutions, and gave me the wisdom and determination I needed to overcome every obstacle.

This verse teaches us that no matter what circumstances we are in, we are not alone. God's presence is our strength, and His power is made perfect in our weakness. When we face trials, we are not meant to walk through them in our own strength. We are called to rely on God's strength, trusting that He will lead us to victory. With God by our side, we cannot fail.

God's promise to never leave us is a declaration of His commitment to our success. Whether we're starting a new project, facing an important decision, or simply navigating the challenges of everyday life, we can rest in the assurance that God is with us. He goes before us, prepares the way, and equips us to succeed. Failure is not in His plan for us. He is the one who will give us the wisdom, courage, and perseverance we need to succeed in all that we do.

The key to overcoming fear and doubt is to remember that God is with us. When we feel weak, He is our strength. When we feel afraid, He is our courage. And when we face challenges that seem insurmountable, He is our guide. We can face every situation with confidence because we know that God is by our side, and He will never leave us or forsake us.

So, whatever you may be facing today, remember this: *You are not alone.* God is with you, and with His strength, you cannot fail. Hold fast to the promise of Deuteronomy 31:6 — *"Be strong and courageous. Do not be afraid, for the Lord your God goes with you."* With Him by your side, you can face any challenge, and you will emerge victorious.

"Understanding God's Power: His Will Will Be Done"

Ezekiel 37:4-5 says: *"Then He said to me, 'Prophesy to these bones and say to them, 'Dry bones, hear the word of the Lord! This is what the Sovereign Lord says to these bones: I will make breath enter you, and you will come to life.'"* This passage serves as a powerful reminder that God's ways are beyond our understanding, and His ability to act is not limited by time or space. His power is immeasurable, and when He speaks, His will is accomplished with precision and speed.

God's work is not slow or hindered by human limitations. Ezekiel's vision of the dry bones coming to life demonstrates God's ability to revive, restore, and transform even the most hopeless situations. The dry bones, which seemed lifeless and beyond hope, heard the word of the Lord, and in an instant, they were brought to life. This is the kind of power our God possesses.

Sometimes, when we look at our circumstances, we feel as though things are beyond repair. We see situations that appear hopeless, relationships that seem dead, or dreams that seem too far out of reach. But the message of Ezekiel 37 reminds us that God is not bound by what we see or understand. His power is limitless, and He can change any situation, no matter how impossible it seems.

When God speaks, things happen. The Bible tells us that God's words carry immense power. In the same way that He spoke the world into existence, He can speak life into any circumstance. The verse from Ezekiel demonstrates the immediate and swift action of God's will. The moment He spoke, the bones came together, muscles formed, and breath filled their bodies. There was no delay, no hesitation. God's power is like a force that moves faster than we can comprehend. It is quick, effective, and unstoppable.

God's timing is always perfect, and His plans unfold exactly as He intends. We may not always understand how or when things will happen, but we can trust that God is working on our behalf. The pace at which He works may seem faster or slower than we expect, but we must remember that He is always in control. Just as God could bring life to dry bones in an instant, He can change your situation in ways you may not expect.

God can accomplish anything He sets His mind to, and His promises are never in vain. If He has spoken a word over your life, you can trust that it will come to pass. His will cannot be thwarted. You may have doubts, but God is never uncertain. What He has declared will be done, and it will be done with speed and effectiveness.

It's easy to become discouraged when we don't see the immediate results of our prayers or efforts. We might wonder why things aren't changing, or why God hasn't acted in the way we expected. But we must remember that God's ways are higher than our ways. What seems slow to us is not slow to God. He is always working, and when the time is right, His plans will unfold perfectly. He doesn't need our help to make things happen. All we need to do is trust and believe that He is at work.

We must trust that God will do exactly what He said He would do. His timing may not be the same as ours, but His actions are always perfect. When we understand this, we can rest in the assurance that God is in control of every detail of our lives.

Just as Ezekiel prophesied to the dry bones, we too can speak God's promises over our lives, knowing that He is able to bring them to pass. We don't need to worry or doubt — God is able. He is the God who can bring life where there is death, hope where there is despair, and restoration where there is brokenness. His power is limitless, and His will will always be accomplished.

So, when you find yourself in a situation that seems impossible, remember Ezekiel 37. Know that God's power is not limited by your circumstances. Trust that He is able to work swiftly and effectively. His word is powerful, and when He speaks, things change. Don't worry about how or when it will happen. What matters is that God has spoken, and His will will come to pass.

God is always at work. He is the one who can bring life to dry bones and hope to hopeless situations. So, trust in His power and His timing. He will do what He has promised, and He will do it with unmatched speed and perfection.

"Seek God's Kingdom Above All Else"

In life, we often find ourselves consumed with desires — the need for success, the craving for approval, the longing for material wealth, or the constant pursuit of comfort and pleasure. These desires are natural, but they can easily become distractions that take us away from the higher purpose we were created for. When we focus solely on our own desires, we forget to look at the bigger picture — God's kingdom and His will for our lives.

Matthew 6:33 encourages us to live with a different perspective: *"But seek first His kingdom and His righteousness, and all these things will be given to you as well."* This verse teaches us that when we make God our priority, when we place His desires above our own, everything else will fall into place. Instead of striving for things that are temporary, we are called to focus on the eternal — the pursuit of God's kingdom, His will, and His glory.

The world teaches us to chase after fame, fortune, and success. It tells us that these things are what will bring us happiness and fulfillment. But in reality, these things are fleeting. They are like shadows that disappear the moment we think we have grasped them. The truth is, these desires, when placed above God, can lead to frustration, discontent, and a sense of emptiness.

When we let go of our selfish desires and seek God's kingdom instead, we align ourselves with His purpose. We begin to understand that our true fulfillment comes not from acquiring things, but from serving Him and living for His glory. When we seek His righteousness and His kingdom first, our hearts are transformed. Our desires change. We no longer chase after fleeting pleasures but instead pursue what is eternal and life-giving.

God knows our hearts. He knows what we truly need, even before we ask. He is a loving Father who understands our deepest desires, and He is faithful to provide for us. When we place Him at the center of our lives, He takes care of everything else. We don't need to worry about what we will eat, what we will wear, or how we will succeed. As the Bible promises, God will supply all our needs according to His riches in glory (Philippians 4:19).

There was a time in my life when I was overwhelmed with the pressures of work, family, and personal goals. I was constantly chasing after success, thinking that if I just achieved more, I would find peace and happiness. But the more I pursued these goals, the more I felt drained and unfulfilled. It was then that I realized that my focus was all wrong. I had placed my desires above God's will, and it left me feeling empty.

I began to pray and ask God to help me shift my focus. I made a conscious decision to seek His kingdom first. I started dedicating my time, energy, and efforts to serving Him and pursuing His righteousness. I stopped worrying about what I didn't have and focused on what I could give to God. It wasn't an easy shift, but as I began to align myself with His will, I noticed a change in my heart. I felt a peace that I had never experienced before, knowing that God was in control and that He would provide for all my needs.

When we focus on God's kingdom, we are not only seeking eternal rewards, but we are also bringing His kingdom to earth. Our lives become a reflection of His love, grace, and goodness. We become a light in the darkness, showing others the way to His truth. When we make God our priority, our lives take on new purpose and meaning.

God is not just a provider; He is our Father. He knows our hearts, He understands our needs, and He cares deeply for us. When we trust Him with our desires and our lives, we can be confident that He will never fail us. He will provide everything we need and more — not just in the material sense, but in the peace, joy, and fulfillment that comes from living in relationship with Him.

So, if you are feeling overwhelmed or restless, take a moment to step back and refocus. Let go of the pressure to achieve everything on your own and turn your heart towards God. Seek His kingdom, seek His righteousness, and trust that He will take care of the rest. When we make God our priority, everything else falls into place. He is our Provider, our Protector, and our Savior. He knows exactly what we need, and He will supply all our needs in His perfect timing.

Remember, when we seek God with all our hearts, He will satisfy us in ways we never imagined. His love is deeper than any earthly desire, and His plans for us are greater than anything we can imagine. Seek Him first, and trust that He will take care of the rest. He is the One who knows us

better than we know ourselves, and He will provide exactly
what we need — today and always